IT'S NOT ABOUT ME

Rescue from the Life We Thought Would Make Us Happy

MAX LUCADO

THOMAS NELSON
Since 1798

NASHVILLE DALLAS MEXICO CITY RIO DE JANEIRO

Published in Nashville, Tennessee, by Thomas Nelson. Thomas Nelson is a registered trademark of Thomas Nelson, Inc.

Thomas Nelson, Inc., titles may be purchased in bulk for educational, business, fund-raising, or sales promotional use. For information, please e-mail SpecialMarkets@thomasnelson.com.

Unless otherwise indicated, Scripture quotations used in this book are from the New American Standard Bible®, © 1960, 1977, 1995 by the Lockman Foundation. Other Scripture references are from the following sources: The Contemporary English Version (CEV) © 1991 by the American Bible Society. Used by permission. The Holy Bible, English Standard Version (ESV), © 2001 by Crossway Bibles, a division of Good News Publishers. Used by permission. All rights reserved. The Jerusalem Bible (JB), © 1966, 1967 and 1968 by Darton, Longman & Todd Ltd and Doubleday, a division of Random House, Inc. All rights reserved. The King James Version of the Bible (KJV). The Living Bible (TLB), © 1971 by Tyndale House Publishers, Wheaton, Ill. Used by permission. The Message (MSG), © 1993. Used by permission of NavPress Publishing Group. The New Century Version (NCV), © 2005 by Thomas Nelson, Inc. Used by permission. All rights reserved. The Holy Bible, New International Version® (NIV). © 1973, 1978, 1983, International Bible Society. Used by permission of Zondervan Bible Publishers. The New King James Version® (NKJV), © 1982 by Thomas Nelson, Inc. Used by permission. All rights reserved. The Holy Bible, New Living Translation (NLT), © 1996. Used by permission of Tyndale House Publishers, Inc., Wheaton, Illinois 60189. All rights reserved. J. B. Phillips: The New Testament in Modern English, Revised Edition (PHILLIPS). © J. B. Phillips 1958, 1960, 1972. Used by permission of Macmillan Publishing Co., Inc. The Revised Standard Version of the Bible (RSV), © 1946, 1952, and 1971 by the Division of Christian Education of the National Council of the Churches of Christ in the USA. Used by permission.

ISBN: 978-0-8499-4664-6 (SE)

Library of Congress Cataloging-in-Publication Data

Lucado, Max.
   It's not about me : rescue from the life we thought would make us happy / Max Lucado.
     p. cm.
ISBN: 978-1-5914-5042-9
ISBN: 978-1-5914-5169-3 (IE)
   1. Man (Christian theology) I. Title.
   BT701.3.L83 2004
   248.4—dc22

2003021164

Printed in the United States of America
10 11 12 13 WOR 6 5 4 3 2 1

TO KENNY AND SHARON WILSON

THERE MAY BE A FINER COUPLE ON THIS EARTH,
BUT I HAVEN'T MET THEM.
FOR YOUR FRIENDSHIP, FAITH, AND
FAR TOO FEW HAMBURGERS,
DENALYN AND I SAY THANK YOU.
WE GLADLY DEDICATE THIS BOOK TO YOU:
TWO PEOPLE WHO, BECAUSE YOU ALREADY LIVE IT,
DON'T NEED TO READ IT.

CONTENTS

ACKNOWLEDGMENTS

On a summer day in the late nineties I ran into a friend in a hotel lobby. Our last visit had occurred a year earlier. He had a few minutes. I had an empty stomach. So we bought deli sandwiches, found a table, and took a seat. "What has God been teaching you this year?" My question was expectation-free. But his answer gave me more than a sandwich to chew on.

"What has he been teaching me this year?" he reflected. "He's been teaching me that: It's not about me."

The phrase stirred enough reflections to become a series of messages and, eventually, this book. So it's only right for me to pause and salute Sealy Yates. Thanks for sharing the line. More important, thanks for modeling it.

Sealy is not the only one who made this work possible. Here are some others:

Liz Heaney and Karen Hill—You so skillfully and gently recraft, clarify. Thanks to you, this book, and the one who wrote it, are in better shape.

Steve and Cheryl Green—Thanks for superintending my life and being our friends. Your comradeship means more to me than I can say.

Byron Williamson, Joey Paul, and the entire Integrity team—Congratulations on the launch. Honored to be aboard.

My Peak of the Week family—You let me guinea pig this material on you. How kind you were to stay awake.

Carol Bartley—No one does it better. Your penchant for grammatical precision astounds us all.

Dwight Edwards—*Revolution Within* connected the dots for me.

John Piper—Reading *The Supremacy of God in Preaching* was like seeing a map of the solar system for the first time. Thanks for reminding me of my place.

Dean Merrill—Thanks for graciously squaring the facts.

Rick Atchley—Thanks for the great messages, for being a great friend.

Charles Prince—Thanks for untangling theological knots and sharing a lifetime of knowledge.

Jenna, Andrea, and Sara—my daughters, my treasures.

Denalyn, my wife—Vienna had Mozart. I have you. What music you bring into my life.

And most of all to you, Author of life. What a great God you are. It's all about you. Period.

But all of us who are Christians . . .
reflect like mirrors the glory of the Lord.

2 Corinthians 3:18 PHILLIPS

FOREWORD

NBA championship teams have something in common: they play with one goal in mind. Each player contributes his own gifts and efforts so that the greater goal—winning—can be reached. But players who seek their own glory at the sacrifice of the team's glory drive the team away from success. So it is with life. The goal is not our own glory. In fact, trying to make life "all about us" pushes happiness further out of reach.

Our society is not wired for this kind of thinking. It's a "me-centric" world out there, which destroys much of what should be good. Marriages are ruined because one or both partners are focused on their own happiness. Successful men and women are ruined by their own success, believing they don't need anyone else's input. And for some, life's troubles are magnified because they believe life is all about them.

The Bible is full of men and women who struggled with "me-centric" thinking, so our generation is not alone. If we would learn from them, we could live in freedom. We would be able to enjoy our successes without taking the credit, like King David. We could bear up under troubles with confidence in God, like Job. By letting go of our own agendas and time-tables, as Moses finally did, we would discover that God's plans are mind-blowing. In the end, a "God-centric" lifestyle would free us to live life to the fullest!

My friend Max Lucado has years of experience in following God, which is why I am happy to recommend this book. If you want a great meal, I'll send you to a great chef. But if you want to learn about God's ways, I'll send you to someone who has walked with him for a long while.

Max is such a man; the Lord has prepared him for just this purpose. I encourage you to read with an open heart as Max shares the joy of a God-centered life.

May God free us all from "me-centric" living. All the glory is His!

—*David Robinson*
Former NBA Player

CHAPTER ONE

BUMPING LIFE
OFF SELF-CENTER

1

Blame the bump on Copernicus.

Until Copernicus came along in 1543, we earthlings enjoyed center stage. Fathers could place an arm around their children, point to the night sky, and proclaim, "The universe revolves around us."

Ah, the hub of the planetary wheel, the navel of the heavenly body, the 1600 Pennsylvania Avenue of the cosmos. Ptolemy's second-century finding convinced us. Stick a pin in the center of the stellar map, and you've found the earth. Dead center.

And, what's more, dead still! Let the other planets vagabond through the skies. Not us. No sir. We stay put. As predictable as Christmas. No orbiting. No rotating. Some fickle planets revolve 180 degrees from one day to the next. Not ours. As budgeless as the Rock of Gibraltar. Let's hear loud applause for the earth, the anchor of the universe.

But then came Nicolaus. Nicolaus Copernicus with his

maps, drawings, bony nose, Polish accent, and pestering questions. Oh, those questions he asked.

"Ahem, can anyone tell me what causes the seasons to change?"

"Why do some stars appear in the day and others at night?"

"Does anyone know exactly how far ships can sail before falling off the edge of the earth?"

"Trivialities!" people scoffed. "Who has time for such problems? Smile and wave, everyone. Heaven's homecoming queen has more pressing matters to which to attend."

But Copernicus persisted. He tapped our collective shoulders and cleared his throat. "Forgive my proclamation, but," and pointing a lone finger toward the sun, he announced, "behold the center of the solar system."

People denied the facts for over half a century. When like-minded Galileo came along, the throne locked him up, and the church kicked him out. You'd have thought he had called the king a stepchild or the pope a Baptist.

People didn't take well to demotions back then.

We still don't.

What Copernicus did for the earth, God does for our souls. Tapping the collective shoulder of humanity, he points to the Son—his Son—and says, "Behold the center of it all."

"God raised him [Christ] from death and set him on a

throne in deep heaven, in charge of running the universe, everything from galaxies to governments, no name and no power exempt from his rule. And not just for the time being but *forever*. He is in charge of it all, has the final word on everything. At the center of all this, Christ rules the church" (Ephesians 1:20–22 MSG).

When God looks at the center of the universe, he doesn't look at you. When heaven's stagehands direct the spotlight toward the star of the show, I need no sunglasses. No light falls on me.

Lesser orbs, that's us. Appreciated. Valued. Loved dearly. But central? Essential? Pivotal? Nope. Sorry. Contrary to the Ptolemy within us, the world does not revolve around us. Our comfort is not God's priority. If it is, something's gone awry. If we are the marquee event, how do we explain flat-earth challenges like death, disease, slumping economies, or rumbling earthquakes? If God exists to please us, then shouldn't we always be pleased?

> WHAT COPERNICUS DID FOR THE EARTH, GOD DOES FOR OUR SOULS.

Could a Copernican shift be in order? Perhaps our place is

not at the center of the universe. God does not exist to make a big deal out of us. We exist to make a big deal out of him. It's not about you. It's not about me. It's all about him.

The moon models our role.

What does the moon do? She generates no light. Contrary to the lyrics of the song, this harvest moon cannot shine on. Apart from the sun, the moon is nothing more than a pitch-black, pockmarked rock. But properly positioned, the moon beams. Let her do what she was made to do, and a clod of dirt becomes a source of inspiration, yea, verily, romance. The moon reflects the greater light.

And she's happy to do so! You never hear the moon complaining. She makes no waves about making waves. Let the cow jump over her or astronauts step on her; she never objects. Even though sunning is accepted while mooning is the butt of bad jokes, you won't hear ol' Cheeseface grumble. The moon is at peace in her place. And because she is, soft light touches a dark earth.

What would happen if we accepted our place as Son reflectors?

Such a shift comes so stubbornly, however. We've been demanding our way and stamping our feet since infancy. Aren't we all born with a default drive set on selfishness? *I want a spouse who makes me happy and coworkers who always ask my opin-*

ion. I want weather that suits me and traffic that helps me and a government that serves me. It is all about me. We relate to the advertisement that headlined, "For the man who thinks the world revolves around him." A prominent actress justified her appearance in a porn magazine by saying, "I wanted to express myself."

Self-promotion. Self-preservation. Selfcenteredness. It's all about me!

They all told us it was, didn't they? Weren't we urged to look out for number one? Find our place in the sun? Make a name for ourselves? We thought self-celebration would make us happy . . .

But what chaos this philosophy creates. What if a symphony orchestra followed such an approach? Can you imagine an orchestra with an "It's all about me" outlook? Each artist clamoring for self-expression. Tubas blasting nonstop. Percussionists pounding to get attention. The cellist shoving the flutist out of the center-stage chair. The trumpeter standing atop the conductor's stool tooting his horn. Sheet music disregarded. Conductor ignored. What do you have but an endless tune-up session!

Harmony? Hardly.

Happiness? Are the musicians happy to be in the group? Not at all. Who enjoys contributing to a cacophony?

You don't. We don't. We were not made to live this way. But aren't we guilty of doing just that?

No wonder our homes are so noisy, businesses so stress-filled, government so cutthroat, and harmony so rare. If you think it's all about you, and I think it's all about me, we have no hope for a melody. We've chased so many skinny rabbits that we've missed the fat one: the God-centered life.

THE GOD-CENTERED LIFE WORKS. AND IT RESCUES US FROM A LIFE THAT DOESN'T.

What would happen if we took our places and played our parts? If we played the music the Maestro gave us to play? If we made his song our highest priority?

Would we see a change in families? We'd certainly *hear* a change. Less "Here is what I want!" More "What do you suppose God wants?"

What if a businessman took that approach? Goals of money and name making, he'd shelve. God-reflecting would dominate.

And your body? Ptolemaic thinking says, "It's mine; I'm going to enjoy it." God-centered thinking acknowledges, "It's God's; I have to respect it."

We'd see our suffering differently. "My pain proves God's absence" would be replaced with "My pain expands God's purpose."

Talk about a Copernican shift. Talk about a healthy shift.

Life makes sense when we accept our place. The gift of pleasures, the purpose of problems—all for him. The God-centered life works. And it rescues us from a life that doesn't.

But how do we make the shift? How can we be bumped off self-center? Attend a seminar, howl at the moon, read a Lucado book? None of these (though the author appreciates that last idea). We move from me-focus to God-focus by pondering him. Witnessing him. Following the counsel of the apostle Paul: "Beholding as in a glass the glory of the Lord, [we] are changed into the same image from glory to glory, even as by the Spirit of the Lord" (2 Corinthians 3:18 KJV).

Beholding him changes us. Couldn't we use a change? Let's give it a go. Who knows? We might just discover our place in the universe.

PART ONE

GOD-PONDERING

CHAPTER TWO

SHOW ME
YOUR GLORY

2

An anxious Moses pleads for help. "[God], you tell me, 'Lead this people,' but you don't let me know whom you're going to send with me. . . . Are you traveling with us or not?" (Exodus 33:12, 16 MSG).

You can hardly fault his fears. Encircled first by Israelites who long for Egypt, and second by a desert of hot winds and blazing boulders, the ex-shepherd needs assurance. His Maker offers it. "I myself will go with you. . . . I will do what you ask, because I know you very well, and I am pleased with you" (vv. 14, 17 NCV).

You'd think that would have been enough for Moses, but he lingers. Thinking, perhaps, of that last sentence, "I will do what you ask . . ." Perhaps God will indulge one more request. So he swallows, sighs, and requests . . .

For what do you think he will ask? He has God's attention. God seems willing to hear his prayer. "The LORD spoke to Moses face to face as a man speaks with his friend" (v. 11 NCV).

15

The patriarch senses an opportunity to ask for anything. What request will he make?

So many requests he could make. How about a million requests? That's how many adults are in Moses' rearview mirror (Exodus 12:37). A million stiff-necked, unappreciative, cow-worshiping ex-slaves who grumble with every step. Had Moses prayed, "Could you turn these people into sheep?" who would have blamed him?

Sheep. Only a few months before, Moses was in this same desert, near this same mountain, keeping an eye on a flock. What a difference this time around. Sheep don't make demands in a desert or a mess out of blessings. And they certainly don't make calves out of gold or ask to go back to Egypt.

And what about Israel's enemies? Battlefields lie ahead. Combat with Hittites, Jebusites . . . Termites, and Cellulites. They infest the land. Can Moses mold an army out of pyramid-building Hebrews?

I will do what you ask . . .

"Could you just beam us to Canaan?"

Moses knew what God could do. The entire Ancient East knew. They were still talking about Aaron's staff becoming a snake and the Nile becoming blood. Air so thick with gnats you breathed them. Ground so layered with locusts you crunched them. Noonday blackness. Hail-pounded crops.

16

Flesh landscaped with boils. Funerals for the firstborn.

God turned the Red Sea into a red carpet. Manna fell. Quail ran. Water bubbled from within a rock. God can move mountains.

In fact, he moved the very mountain of Sinai on which Moses stood. When God spoke, Sinai shook, and Moses' knees followed suit. Moses knew what God could do.

Worse, he knew what these people were prone to do.

Moses found them dancing around a golden calf, their memories of God as stale as yesterday's manna. He carried the handwriting of God on a stone, and the Israelites were worshiping a heartless farm animal.

WHEN OUR DEEPEST DESIRE IS NOT THE THINGS OF GOD, OR A FAVOR FROM GOD, BUT GOD HIMSELF, WE CROSS A THRESHOLD.

It was more than Moses could take. He melted the metal cow and pounded the gold into dust and forced the worshipers to drink up.

God was ready to be done with them and start over with Moses as he had done with Noah. But twice Moses pleads for mercy, and twice mercy is extended (Exodus 32:11–14, 31–32).

And God, touched by Moses' heart, hears Moses' prayer. "My presence will go with you. I'll see the journey to the end" (Exodus 33:14 MSG).

But Moses needs more. One more request. Glory. "Show me your glory" (33:18 NCV).

We cross a line when we make such a request. When our deepest desire is not the things of God, or a favor from God, but God himself, we cross a threshold. Less self-focus, more God-focus. Less about me, more about him.

"Show me your radiance," Moses is praying. "Flex your biceps. Let me see the *S* on your chest. Your preeminence. Your heart-stopping, ground-shaking extraspectacularness. Forget the money and the power. Bypass the youth. I can live with an aging body, but I can't live without you. I want more God, please. I'd like to see more of your glory."

Why did Moses want to see God's greatness?

Ask yourself a similar question. Why do you stare at sunsets and ponder the summer night sky? Why do you search for a rainbow in the mist or gaze at the Grand Canyon? Why do you allow the Pacific surf to mesmerize and Niagara to hypnotize? How do we explain our fascination with such sights?

Beauty? Yes. But doesn't the beauty point to a beautiful Someone? Doesn't the immensity of the ocean suggest an immense Creator? Doesn't the rhythm of migrating cranes and beluga whales hint of a brilliant mind? And isn't that what we desire? A beautiful Maker? An immense Creator? A God so mighty that he can commission the birds and command the fish?

"Show me your glory, God," Moses begs. Forget a bank; he wants to see Fort Knox. He needs a walk in the vault of God's wealth. *Would you stun me with your strength? Numb me with your wisdom? Steal my breath with a brush of yours? A moment in the spray of the cataract of grace, a glimpse of your glory, God.* This is the prayer of Moses.

And God answers it. He places his servant in the cleft of a rock, telling Moses: "You cannot see My face; for no man shall see Me, and live. . . . I . . . will cover you with My hand while I pass by. Then I will take away My hand, and you shall see My back; but My face shall not be seen" (Exodus 33:20, 22–23 NKJV).

And so Moses, cowering beneath the umbrella of God's palm, waits, surely with face bowed, eyes covered, and pulse racing, until God gives the signal. When the hand lifts, Moses' eyes do the same and catch a distant, disappearing glance of the back parts of God. The heart and center of the Maker is too much for Moses to bear. A fading glimpse will have to do. I'm seeing the long gray hair of Moses wind-whipped forward and his leathery hand grabbing a rock in the wall lest he fall. And as the gust settles and his locks rest again on his shoulders, we

IT'S NOT ABOUT ME

see the impact. His face. Gleaming. Bright as if backlit by a thousand torches. Unknown to Moses, but undeniable to the Hebrews, is his shimmering face. When he descended the mountain, "the sons of Israel could not look intently at the face of Moses because of the glory of his face" (2 Corinthians 3:7).

Witnesses saw, not anger in his jaw, or worry in his eyes, or a scowl on his lips; they saw God's glory in his face.

Did he have reason for anger? Cause for worry? Of course. Challenges await him. A desert and forty years of great challenges. But now, having seen God's face, he can face them.

Forgive my effrontery, but shouldn't Moses' request be yours? You've got problems. Look at you. Living in a dying body, walking on a decaying planet, surrounded by a self-centered society. Some saved by grace; others fueled by narcissism. Many of us by both. Cancer. War. Disease.

These are no small issues. A small god? No thanks. You and I need what Moses needed—a glimpse of God's glory. Such a sighting can change you forever.

In the early pages of my childhood memory, I see this picture. My father and I sit side by side in a chapel. We both wear our only suits. The shirt collar rubs my neck; the pew feels hard to my bottom; the sight of my dead uncle leaves us all silent. This is my first funeral. My nine years of life have not prepared me for death. What I see unnerves me. Aunts, typically jovial and talkative, weep loudly. Uncles, commonly quick with a word and joke, stare wide eyed at the casket. And Buck, my big uncle with meaty hands, big belly, and booming voice, lies whitish and waxy in the coffin.

I remember my palms moistening and my heart bouncing in my chest like tennis sneakers in a clothes dryer. Fear had me in her talons. What other emotion

YOU AND I NEED WHAT MOSES NEEDED— A GLIMPSE OF GOD'S GLORY.

could I feel? Where do I look? The weeping ladies frighten me. Glassy-eyed men puzzle me. My dead uncle spooks me. But then I look up. I see my father.

He turns his face toward me and smiles softly. "It's okay, son," he assures, laying a large hand on my leg. Somehow I know it is. Why it is, I don't know. My family still wails. Uncle Buck is still dead. But if Dad, in the midst of it all, says it's okay, then that's enough.

At that moment I realized something. I could look around and find fear, or look at my father and find faith.

I chose my father's face.

So did Moses.

So can you.

DIVINE
SELF-PROMOTION

3

Moses asked to see it on Sinai.

It billowed through the temple, leaving priests too stunned to minister.

When Ezekiel saw it, he had to bow.

It encircled the angels and starstruck the shepherds in the Bethlehem pasture.

Jesus radiates it.

John beheld it.

Peter witnessed it on Transfiguration Hill.

Christ will return enthroned in it.

Heaven will be illuminated by it.[1]

It gulfstreams the Atlantic of Scripture, touching every person with the potential of changing every life. Including yours. One glimpse, one taste, one sampling, and your faith will never be the same . . .

Glory.

God's glory.

To seek God's glory is to pray, "Thicken the air with your presence; make it misty with your majesty. Part heaven's drapes, and let your nature spill forth. God, show us God."

> TO SEEK GOD'S GLORY IS TO PRAY, "LET YOUR NATURE SPILL FORTH. GOD, SHOW US GOD."

What the word *Alps* does for the mountains of Europe, *glory* does for God's nature. *Alps* encompasses a host of beauties: creeks, peaks, falling leaves, running elk. To ask to see the Alps is to ask to see it all. To ask to see God's glory is to ask to see all of God. God's glory carries the full weight of his attributes: his love, his character, his strength, and on and on.

David celebrated God's glory.

Bravo, GOD, bravo!
Gods and all angels shout, "Encore!"
In awe before the glory,
in awe before God's visible power.
Stand at attention!
Dress your best to honor him!

GOD thunders across the waters,
Brilliant, his voice and his face, streaming brightness—
GOD, across the flood waters.

GOD's thunder tympanic,
GOD's thunder symphonic.

GOD's thunder smashes cedars,
GOD topples the northern cedars.

The mountain ranges skip like spring colts,
The high ridges jump like wild kid goats.

GOD's thunder spits fire.
GOD thunders, the wilderness quakes;
He makes the desert of Kadesh shake.

GOD's thunder sets the oak trees dancing
A wild dance, whirling; the pelting rain strips their branches.
We fall to our knees—we call out, "Glory!"
(Psalm 29:1–9 MSG)

The word signals high honor. The Hebrew term for *glory* descends from a root word meaning heavy, weighty, or important. God's glory, then, celebrates his significance, his uniqueness, his one-of-a-kindness. As Moses prayed, "Who among the gods is like you, O LORD? Who is like you—majestic in holiness, awesome in glory, working wonders?" (Exodus 15:11 NIV).

When you think "God's glory," think "preeminence." And, when you think "preeminence," think "priority." For God's glory is God's priority.

God's staff meetings, if he had them, would revolve around one question: "How can we reveal my glory today?" God's to-do list consists of one item: "Reveal my glory." Heaven's framed and mounted purpose statement hangs in the angels' break room just above the angel food cake. It reads: "Declare God's glory."

God exists to showcase God.

He told Moses: "By those who come near Me I must be regarded as holy; and before all the people I must be glorified" (Leviticus 10:3 NKJV).

Why did he harden Pharaoh's heart? "I will harden Pharaoh's heart, and he will pursue them [the Israelites]. But I will gain glory for myself through Pharaoh and all his army, and the Egyptians will know that I am the LORD" (Exodus 14:4 NIV).

Why do the heavens exist? The heavens exist to "declare the glory of God" (Psalm 19:1 NIV).

Why did God choose the Israelites? Through Isaiah he called out to "everyone who is called by My name, whom I have created for My glory" (Isaiah 43:7 NKJV).

Why do people struggle? God answers, "I have tested you in the furnace of affliction. For My own sake, for My own sake, I will act" (Isaiah 48:10–11). "Trust me in your times of trouble, and I will rescue you, and you will give me glory" (Psalm 50:15 NLT).

> EVERY ACT OF HEAVEN REVEALS GOD'S GLORY. EVERY ACT OF JESUS DID THE SAME.

He spoke of "this people I have formed for Myself; they shall declare My praise" (Isaiah 43:21 NKJV).

The prophet Isaiah proclaimed, "You lead Your people, to make Yourself a glorious name" (Isaiah 63:14 NKJV).

Christ taught us to make God's reputation our priority in prayer: "Our Father who is in heaven, hallowed be Your name" (Matthew 6:9).

Every act of heaven reveals God's glory. Every act of Jesus did the same. Indeed, "The Son reflects the glory of God" (Hebrews 1:3 NCV). The night before his crucifixion, Jesus declared, "Now my heart is troubled, and what shall I say? 'Father, save me from this hour'? No, it was for this very reason

I came to this hour. Father, glorify your name!" (John 12:27–28 NIV). Paul explains that "Christ has become a servant of the Jews . . . so that the Gentiles may glorify God for his mercy" (Romans 15:8–9 NIV).

And Jesus declared his mission a success by saying, "I have brought you glory on earth by completing the work you gave me to do" (John 17:4 NIV).

God has one goal: God. "I have my reputation to keep up" (Isaiah 48:11 MSG).

Surprised? Isn't such an attitude, dare we ask, self-centered? Don't we deem this behavior "self-promotion"? Why does God broadcast himself?

For the same reason the pilot of the lifeboat does. Think of it this way. You're floundering neck-deep in a dark, cold sea. Ship sinking. Life jacket deflating. Strength waning. Through the inky night comes the voice of a lifeboat pilot. But you cannot see him. What do you want the driver of the lifeboat to do?

Be quiet? Say nothing? Stealth his way through the drowning passengers? By no means! You need volume! Amp it up, buddy! In biblical jargon, you want him to show his glory. You need to hear him say, "I am here. I am strong. I have room for you. I can save you!" Drowning passengers want the pilot to reveal his preeminence.

Don't we want God to do the same? Look around. People

thrash about in seas of guilt, anger, despair. Life isn't working. We are going down fast. But God can rescue us. And only one message matters. His! We need to see God's glory.

Make no mistake. God has no ego problem. *He does not reveal his glory for his good. We need to witness it for ours.* We need a strong hand to pull us into a safe boat. And, once aboard, what becomes our priority?

> HE DOES NOT REVEAL HIS GLORY FOR HIS GOOD. WE NEED TO WITNESS IT FOR OURS.

Simple. Promote God. We declare his preeminence. "Hey! Strong boat over here! Able pilot! He can pull you out!"

Passengers promote the pilot. "Not to us, O LORD, not to us, but to Your name give glory because of Your loving-kindness, because of Your truth" (Psalm 115:1). If we boast at all, we "boast in the Lord" (2 Corinthians 10:17).

The breath you took as you read that last sentence was given to you for one reason, that you might for another moment "reflect the Lord's glory" (2 Corinthians 3:18 NIV). God awoke you and me this morning for one purpose: "Declare his glory among the nations, his marvelous deeds among all peoples" (1 Chronicles 16:24 NIV).

"God made all things, and everything continues through

him and *for* him. To him be the glory forever" (Romans 11:36 NCV, emphasis mine). "There is only one God, the Father, who created everything, and *we exist for him*" (1 Corinthians 8:6 NLT, emphasis mine).

Why does the earth spin? For him.

Why do you have talents and abilities? For him.

Why do you have money or poverty? For him.

Strength or struggles? For him.

Everything and everyone exists to reveal his glory.

Including you.

CHAPTER FOUR

HOLY DIFFERENT

4

John Hanning Speke stands on the river edge and stares at the wall of water. He has dedicated the better part of 1858 to getting here. For weeks he and his party slashed through African brush and forded deep rivers. Natives bearing iron-headed spears pursued them. Crocodiles and sterns kept an eye on them. But finally, after miles of jungle marching and grass plodding, they found the falls.

Only a Britisher could so clearly understate the sight. "We were well rewarded," he wrote in his journal.

The roar of the waters, the thousands of passenger fish, leaping at the falls with all their might, the Wasoga and Waganda fishermen coming out in boats and taking post on all the rocks with rod and hook, hippopotami and crocodiles lying sleepily on the water . . . made in all, as interesting a picture as one would want to see.[1]

Speke could not leave. He sketched the sight over and over. He dedicated an entire day to simply staring at the majesty of the falls at the upper Nile. Not hard to understand why. No region of England boasted any such sight. Rarely do eyes fall on a hitherto unseen image. Speke's did. And he was stunned by what he saw.

Fourteen years later, halfway around the globe, Frederick Dellenbaugh was equally impressed. He was only eighteen when he joined Major Powell on his pioneering river voyages through the Grand Canyon. Led by the one-armed Powell, the explorers floated on leaky boats and faced high waters. It's a wonder they survived. It's every bit as much a wonder what they saw. Dellenbaugh described the scene:

My back being towards the fall I could not see it. . . . Nearer and nearer came the angry tumult; the Major shouted "Back water!" there was a sudden dropping away of all support; then the mighty wavers [*sic*] smote us. The boat rose to them well, but we were flying at twenty-five miles an hour and at every leap the breakers rolled over us. "Bail!" shouted the Major,—"Bail for your lives!" and we dropped the oars to bail, though bailing was almost useless. . . . The boat rolled and pitched like a ship in a tornado.

... canopies of foam pour[ed] over gigantic black boulders, first on one side, then on the other. . . . If you will take a watch and count by it ninety seconds, you will probably have about the time we were in this chaos, though it seemed much longer to me. Then we were through.[2]

Young Dellenbaugh knew rapids. Rivers and raging water were not new to him. But something about this river was. The sudden immensity, stark intensity—something stole the oarsman's breath. He knew rapids. But none like this.

Speke, speechless. Dellenbaugh, drenched and awestruck.

And Isaiah, facefirst on the temple floor. Arms crossed above his head, muffled voice crying for mercy. Like the explorers, he's just seen the unseen. But unlike the explorers, he's seen more than creation—he's seen the Creator. He's seen God.

Seven and one-half centuries before Christ, Isaiah was ancient Israel's version of a Senate chaplain or court priest. His family, aristocratic. His Hebrew, impeccable. Polished, professional, and successful. But the day he saw God only one response seemed appropriate: "Woe is me, for I am ruined." What caused such a confession? What stirred such a reply? The answer is found in the thrice-repeated words of the seraphim: "Holy, holy, holy."

Seraphim stood above Him, each having six wings: with two he covered his face, and with two he covered his feet, and with two he flew. And one called out to another and said,

"Holy, Holy, Holy, is the LORD of hosts,

The whole earth is full of His glory."

And the foundations of the thresholds trembled at the voice of him who called out, while the temple was filling with smoke. Then I said,

"Woe is me, for I am ruined!

Because I am a man of unclean lips,

And I live among a people of unclean lips;

For my eyes have seen the King, the LORD of hosts."

(Isaiah 6:2–5)

On the one occasion seraphim appear in Scripture, they endlessly trilogize the same word. "Holy, holy, holy is the LORD Almighty" (NIV). Repetition, in Hebrew, performs the work of our highlighter. A tool of emphasis. God, proclaims the six-winged angels, is not holy. He is not holy, holy. He is holy, holy, holy.

What other attribute receives such enforcement? No verse describes God as "wise, wise, wise" or "strong, strong, strong." Only as "holy, holy, holy." God's holiness commands headline attention. The adjective qualifies his name more than all others combined.[3] The first and final songs of the Bible magnify the holiness of God. Having crossed the Red Sea, Moses and the Israelites sang, "Who among the gods is like you, O LORD? Who is like you—majestic in holiness, awesome in glory, working wonders?" (Exodus 15:11 NIV). In Revelation those who had been victorious over the beast sang, "Who will not fear you, O Lord, and bring glory to your name? For you alone are holy" (15:4 NIV).

The Hebrew word for *holy* is *qadosh*, which means cut off or separate. Holiness, then, speaks of the "otherness" of God. His total uniqueness. Everything about God is different from the world he has made.

GOD IS NOT HOLY.

HE IS NOT HOLY, HOLY.

HE IS HOLY, HOLY, HOLY.

What you are to a paper airplane, God is to you. Take a sheet of paper and make one. Contrast yourself with your creation. Challenge it to a spelling contest. Who will win? Dare it to race you around the block. Who is faster? Invite the airplane to a game of one-on-one basketball. Will you not dominate the court?

And well you should. The thing has no brainwaves, no

pulse. It exists only because you formed it and flies only when someone throws it. Multiply the contrasts between you and the paper plane by infinity, and you will begin to catch a glimpse of the disparity between God and us.

To what can we compare God? "Who in the skies is comparable to the LORD? Who among the sons of the mighty is like the LORD?" (Psalm 89:6). "To whom then will you liken God? Or what likeness will you compare with Him?" (Isaiah 40:18).

Even God asks, "To whom will you compare me? Who is my equal?" (Isaiah 40:25 NLT). As if his question needed an answer, he gives one:

I am God—I alone! I am God, and there is no one else like me. Only I can tell you what is going to happen even before it happens. Everything I plan will come to pass, for I do whatever I wish. I will call a swift bird of prey from the east—a leader from a distant land who will come and do my bidding. I have said I would do it, and I will. (Isaiah 46:9–11 NLT)

Any pursuit of God's counterpart is vain. Any search for a godlike person or position on earth is futile. No one and nothing compares with him. No one advises him. No one helps him. It is he who "executes judgment, putting down one and lifting up another" (Psalm 75:7 ESV).

You and I may have power. But God *is* power. We may be a lightning bug, but he is lightning itself. "Wisdom and power are his" (Daniel 2:20 NIV).

Consider the universe around us. Unlike the potter who takes something and reshapes it, God took nothing and created something. God created everything that exists by divine fiat *ex nihilo* (out of nothing). He did not rely on material that was preexistent or coeternal. Prior to creation the universe was not a dark space. The universe did not exist. God even created the darkness. "I am the one who creates the light and makes the darkness" (Isaiah 45:7 NLT). John proclaimed, "You created everything, and it is for your pleasure that they exist and were created" (Revelation 4:11 NLT).

> TRACE THE UNIVERSE BACK TO GOD'S POWER, AND FOLLOW HIS POWER UPSTREAM TO HIS WISDOM.

Trace the universe back to God's power, and follow his

power upstream to his wisdom. God's omniscience governs his omnipotence. Infinite knowledge rules infinite strength. "He is wise in heart, and mighty in strength" (Job 9:4 KJV). "With him is wisdom and strength" (Job 12:13 KJV). "He is mighty in strength and wisdom" (Job 36:5 KJV).

His power is not capricious or careless. Quite the contrary. His wisdom manages and equals his strength. Paul announced, "Oh, the depths of the riches of the wisdom and knowledge of God! How unsearchable his judgments, and his paths beyond tracing out" (Romans 11:33 NIV).

His knowledge about you is as complete as his knowledge about the universe. "Even before a word is on my tongue, behold, O LORD, you know it altogether. . . . Your eyes saw my unformed substance; in your book were written, every one of them, the days that were formed for me, when as yet there were none of them" (Psalm 139:4, 16 ESV).

The veils that block your vision and mine do not block God's. Unspoken words are as if uttered. Unrevealed thoughts are as if proclaimed. Unoccurred moments are as if they were history. He knows the future, the past, the hidden, and the untold. Nothing is concealed from God. He is all-powerful, all-knowing, and all-present.

King David marveled, "Where can I go from Your Spirit? Or where can I flee from Your presence?" (Psalm 139:7). God reminds us, "I am everywhere—both near and far, in heaven and on earth" (Jeremiah 23:23–24 CEV).

See the "holy otherness" of God? In Isaiah's encounter, those who see him most clearly regard him most highly. He is so holy that sinless seraphim cannot bear to look at him! They cover their faces with their wings. They also, oddly, cover their

INFINITE KNOWLEDGE RULES INFINITE STRENGTH.

feet. Why? In He-brew the word for *feet* and the word for *genitalia* are the same.[4] Forgive the thought, but the confession of the angels is that they are absolutely impotent in the presence of God.

Isaiah could relate. When he sees the holiness of God, Isaiah does not boast or swagger. He takes no notes, plans no sermon series, launches no seminar tours. Instead, he falls on his face and begs for mercy. "Woe is me, for I am ruined! Because I am a man of unclean lips, and I live among a people of unclean lips; for my eyes have seen the King, the LORD of hosts" (Isaiah 6:5).

The God-given vision was not about Isaiah but about God and his glory. Isaiah gets the point. "It's not about me. It's all about him." He finds humility, not through seeking it, but through seeking him. One glimpse and the prophet claims citizenship among the infected and diseased—the "unclean," a term used to describe those with leprosy. God's holiness silences human boasting.

And God's mercy makes us holy. Look what happens next.

GOD'S HOLINESS SILENCES HUMAN BOASTING.

Then one of the seraphim flew to me with a burning coal in his hand, which he had taken from the altar with tongs. He touched my mouth with it and said, "Behold, this has touched your lips; and your iniquity is taken away and your sin is forgiven." (Isaiah 6:6–7)

Isaiah makes no request. He asks for no grace. Indeed, he likely assumed mercy was impossible. But God, who is quick to pardon and full of mercy, purges Isaiah of his sin and redirects his life.

God solicits a spokesman. "Whom shall I send, and who will go for Us?" (6:8).

Isaiah's heart and hand shoot skyward. "Here am I. Send me!" (6:8). A glimpse of God's holiness and Isaiah had to speak.

As if he'd found the source of the river, ridden the rage of the canyon. As if he'd seen what Moses had seen—God himself. Albeit a glimpse, but a God-glimpse nonetheless.

And he was different as a result.

Holy different.

JUST A MOMENT

5

Young parents typically rejoice when their children learn new phrases.

"Honey, little Bobby just said bye-bye!"

"Mom, you'll never believe what your granddaughter just did. She counted to five."

Or, "Ernie, tell your uncle what the bird says."

We applaud such moments. I did too.

With one exception.

One phrase my daughter learned gave me pause. Jenna was nearly or barely two years of age, just learning to speak well. With her little hand lost in my big one, we walked through the lobby of our apartment building. Suddenly she stopped. Spotting a ball, she looked up at me and requested, "Just a moment." Sliding her hand from mine, she walked away.

A moment? Who had told her about moments? To date, her existence had been time-free. Toddlers know no beginning

49

or end or hurry or slow or late or soon. The small world of a child amplifies present tense and diminishes future and past. But Jenna's phrase, "Just a moment," announced that time had entered her world.

In his autobiography, *The Sacred Journey,* Frederick Buechner divides his life into three parts: "once below a time," "once above a time," and "beyond time." The childhood years, he says, are lived "once below a time. . . . What child, while summer is happening, bothers to think that summer will end? What child, when snow is on the ground, stops to remember that not long ago the ground was snowless?"[1]

Is childhood for us what life in the Garden was like for Adam and Eve? Before the couple swallowed the line of Satan and the fruit of the tree, no one printed calendars or wore watches or needed cemeteries. They indwelt a time-free world. Minutes passed equally unmeasured in Jenna's two-year-old world. No thought of life being anything different than daily walks and naps and music and Mom and Dad. But "just a moment" belied the intrusion of pirates on her innocent island. Time had invaded her world.

Life, she was discovering, is a cache of moments: measurable and countable increments, like change in a pocket or buttons in a can. Your pocket may be full of decades, my pocket may be down to a few years, but everyone has a certain number of moments.

Everyone, that is, except God. As we list the mind-stretching claims of Christ, let's include this one near the top. "Before Abraham was

NOT EVEN GOD
MADE GOD.

born, I am" (John 8:58). If the mob didn't want to kill Jesus before that sentence, they did afterward. Jesus claimed to be God, the Eternal Being. He identified himself as "the High and Lofty One Who inhabits eternity" (Isaiah 57:15 NKJV).

Scripture broadcasts this attribute in surround-sound. God is "from everlasting" (Psalm 93:2 NKJV) and the "everlasting King" (Jeremiah 10:10 NKJV), "incorruptible" (Romans 1:23 NKJV), "who alone has immortality" (1 Timothy 6:16 NKJV). The heavens and the earth will perish, "but You [O God] are the same, and Your years will have no end" (Psalm 102:27 NKJV). You'll more quickly measure the salt of the ocean than measure the existence of God because "the number of His years is unsearchable" (Job 36:26).

Trace the tree back to a seed. Trace the dress back to a factory. Trace the baby back to a mommy. Trace God back to . . . to . . . to . . .

No one. Not even God made God. "From eternity I am He" (Isaiah 43:13). For that reason we have Jesus making statements such as, "Before Abraham was born, I am" (John 8:58). He didn't say, "Before Abraham was born, *I was*." God never says, "I was," because he still is. He is—right now—in the days of Abraham and in the end of time. He is eternal. He does not live sequential moments, laid out on a time line, one following the other. His world is one moment or, better stated, momentless.

> HE KNOWS YOUR BEGINNING AND YOUR END, BECAUSE HE HAS NEITHER.

He doesn't view history as a progression of centuries but as a single photo. He captures your life, your entire life, in one glance. He sees your birth and burial in one frame. He knows your beginning and your end, because he has neither.

Doesn't make sense, does it? Eternity makes no sense to us, the timebound. You might as well be handed a book written in kanji (unless, of course, you are Japanese). You look at the characters, and all you see is zigzagged lines. You shake your head. This language finds no home in your mind.

But what if someone taught you how to read and write the language? Suppose a native speaker had the time and you had the will so that day by day the symbols that meant nothing to you began to mean something?

With God's help, the same is happening to you and me regarding eternity. He is teaching us the language. "He has also set eternity in their heart" (Ecclesiastes 3:11). Tucked away in each of us is a hunch that we were made for forever and a hope that the hunch is true.

Remember the story of the eagle who was raised by chickens? From the floor of the barnyard she spots an eagle in the clouds, and her heart stirs. "I can do that!" she whispers. The other chickens laugh, but she knows better. She was born different. Born with a belief.

You were too. Your world extends beyond the barnyard of time. A foreverness woos you. Your heavenly life Everests the pebbles of your earthly life. If grains of sand measured the two, how would they stack up? Heaven would be every grain of sand on every beach on earth, plus more. Earthly life, by contrast, would be one hundredth of one grain of sand. Need a phrase to summarize the length of your life on earth? Try Jenna's: "Just a moment."

Wasn't this the phrase of choice for Paul? "Our light affliction, which is *but for a moment,* is working for us a far more exceeding and eternal weight of glory" (2 Corinthians 4:17 NKJV, emphasis mine).

What if we had a glimpse of the apostle as he wrote those words? By this time he had been "beaten times without number, often in danger of death. Five times," he writes, "I received from the Jews thirty-nine lashes. Three times I was beaten with rods, once I was stoned, three times I was shipwrecked, a night and a day I have spent in the deep" (2 Corinthians 11:23–25). He goes on to refer to life-threatening river trips, wilderness wanderings, and exposure to cold, attacks, hunger, and thirst. These, in Paul's words, are light afflictions to be endured for just a moment.

What if we took the same attitude toward life? What if we saw our tough times as a grain of sand scarcely worthy of contrast with the forever dunes?

What if the woman who stopped me the other day would do that? She spoke of seventeen years of a bad marriage. His mistakes, her mistakes. His drinking, her impatience. And now she wants out. After all, her life is blitzing past. If she is going to live, she'd best get busy! Besides, who can assure her that the marriage will work? How does she know that she's not in for two more decades of tough times? She doesn't.

"All about me," counsel says. "Life is short—get out."

God's wisdom, however, says, "Life is short—stay in."

The brevity of life grants power to abide, not an excuse to bail. Fleeting days don't justify fleeing problems. Fleeting days strengthen us to endure problems. Will your problems pass? No guarantee they will. Will your pain cease? Perhaps. Perhaps not. But heaven gives this promise: "our light affliction, which is but for a moment, is working for us a far more exceeding and eternal weight of glory" (2 Corinthians 4:17 NKJV).

The words "weight of glory" conjure up images of the ancient pan scale. Remember the blindfolded lady of justice? She holds a pan scale—two pans, one on either side of the needle. The weight of a purchase would be determined by placing weights on one side and the purchase on the other.

THE BREVITY OF LIFE GRANTS POWER TO ABIDE, NOT AN EXCUSE TO BAIL.

God does the same with your struggles. On one side he stacks all your burdens. Famines. Firings. Parents who forgot you. Bosses who ignored you. Bad breaks, bad health, bad days. Stack them up, and watch one side of the pan scale plummet.

Now witness God's response. Does he remove them? Eliminate the burdens? No, rather than take them, he offsets them. He places an eternal weight of glory on the other side. Endless joy. Measureless peace. An eternity of him. Watch what happens as he sets eternity on your scale.

Everything changes! The burdens lift. The heavy becomes

light when weighed against eternity. If life is "just a moment," can't we endure any challenge for a moment?

We can be sick for *just a moment*.

We can be lonely for *just a moment*.

We can be persecuted for *just a moment*.

We can struggle for *just a moment*.

Can't we?

Can't we wait for our peace? It's not about us anyway. And it's certainly not about now.

HIS UNCHANGING HAND

6

1966. Lyndon Johnson was president. The voices of Goldwater and Dirksen dominated the Senate. Watergate was a D.C. apartment building, and the best known Bush was the one that spoke to Moses. Vietnam rumbled. Hippies rocked. Woodstock was a dairy farm, and the Lucados were moving into a new home.

LBJ soon moved back to Texas, and Watergate snakebit Nixon. Goldwater and Dirksen stepped down, and the Bushes stepped up. Vietnam, hippies, and Woodstock faded like tie-dyed T-shirts, but the Lucado family stayed in that yellow-brick house. For thirty-five years we stayed.

The Beatles came and went. The economy rose and fell and rose again. Much changed, but there was always a Lucado living in the three-bedroom house just off Avenue G.

Until today. As I write, movers load three decades of family life into a truck. The mailman is peeling "Lucado" off the mailbox and stenciling on "Hernandez."

The vacating was bound to happen. It had to happen. But

it's hard to see it happen. Change, like taxes, is necessary but unwelcome.

Change? a few of you are thinking. *You want to talk about change? Let me tell you about change . . .*

Let me tell you about my changing body—Chemotherapists treat my body like a pincushion.

My changing family—We're "Surprise! Pregnant." I'll wear maternity clothes to the high school graduation of my firstborn.

The changing economy—If my investments don't improve, I'll spend my retirement eating macaroni and cheese.

Our changing business—I'm jobless. Mailing resumés pays no bills.

Change. Had more than your share? Wishing you could freeze-frame the video of your world? Would it help to stand in Saint Peter's Square and tell the fellow on the balcony, "Stop! No more change!"?

Save your breath. He can't help. If you're looking for a place with no change, try a soda machine. With life comes change.

With change comes fear, insecurity, sorrow, stress. So what do you do? Hibernate? Take no risks for fear of failing? Give no love for fear of losing? Some opt to. They hold back.

A better idea is to look up. Set your bearings on the one and only North Star in the universe—God. For though life changes, he never does. Scripture makes pupil-popping claims about his permanence.

Consider his strength. Unending. According to Paul, God's power lasts forever (Romans 1:20). His strength never diminishes. Yours and mine will and has. Our energy ebbs and flows more than the Thames River. You aren't as alert in the evening as in the morning. You can't run as fast when you are eighty as when you are twenty. Even the strongest among us must eventually rest. Lance Armstrong can maintain a bike speed of thirty-two mph for a solid hour. Healthy college males last forty-five seconds at that pace. I'd make thirty before wanting to throw up. Armstrong lives up to the last half of his last name. He is strong. But at some point he must rest. His head seeks the pillow, and his body seeks sleep.[1]

Call Jim Eubank strong. Swimming seventy laps a day and holding half a dozen endurance swim records would be proof alone. But still logging a daily mile in the pool and winning races at age eighty-five?[2] Don the Speedo and flex those lats, Mr. Eubank. You are strong, but you won't be strong forever.

God will. The words "I'm feeling strong today" he has never said. He feels equally strong every day.

Daniel calls him "the living God, enduring forever" (Daniel 6:26 ESV). The psalmist tells him, "I will sing of your strength. . . . For you have been to me a fortress and a refuge in the day of my distress. O my Strength, I will sing praises to you, for you, O God, are my fortress, the God who shows me steadfast love" (Psalm 59:16–17 ESV).

Think about it. God never pauses to eat or asks the angels to cover for him while he naps. He never signals a time-out or puts the prayer requests from Russia on hold while he handles South Africa. He "never tires and never sleeps" (Psalm 121:4 NLT). Need a strong hand to hold? You'll always find one in his. His strength never changes.

Need unchanging truth to trust? Try God's. His truth never wavers.

Would that we could say the same. We've learned to season our words with salt, we eat them so often. Our opinions change like Rodeo Drive fashion trends. (Weren't your convictions about child rearing stronger before you had kids? Do you know any Republicans who used to be Democrats and vice versa?) Our convictions tend to change.

Good to know God's don't. His view of right and wrong is the same with you and me as it was with Adam and Eve.

> HE NEVER SIGNALS A TIME-OUT OR PUTS THE PRAYER REQUESTS FROM RUSSIA ON HOLD WHILE HE HANDLES SOUTH AFRICA.

"The word of our God shall stand for ever" (Isaiah 40:8 KJV). "For ever, O LORD, thy word is settled in heaven. . . . All thy commandments are truth. . . . Thou hast founded them for ever" (Psalm 119:89, 151–152 KJV).

Your outlook may change. My convictions may sway, but "the Scripture cannot be broken" (John 10:35 NKJV). And since it can't, since his truth will not waver, God's ways will never alter.

He will always hate sin and love sinners, despise the proud and exalt the humble. He will always convict the evildoer and comfort the heavy-hearted. He never changes direction mid-stream, recalibrates the course midway home, or amends the heavenly Constitution. God will always be the same.

No one else will. Lovers call you today and scorn you tomorrow. Companies follow pay raises with pink slips. Friends applaud you when you drive a classic and dismiss you when you drive a dud. Not God. God is "always the same" (Psalm 102:27 ESV). With him "there is no variation or shadow due to change" (James 1:17 ESV).

Catch God in a bad mood? Won't happen. Fear exhausting his grace? A sardine will swallow the Atlantic first. Think he's given up on you? Wrong. Did he not make a promise to you? "God is not a human being, and he will not lie. He is not a human, and he does not change his mind. What he says he will do, he does. What he promises, he makes come true" (Numbers 23:19 NCV). He's never sullen or sour, sulking or stressed. His strength, truth, ways, and love never change. He is "the same yesterday and today and forever" (Hebrews 13:8 ESV). And because he is, the Lord "will be the stability of your times" (Isaiah 33:6 NKJV).

And couldn't we use some stability? For twenty-seven years the citizens of South Padre trusted the stability of the Queen Isabella Causeway, the longest bridge in Texas. Every day 19,000 motorists used her to travel between Port Isabel and South Padre Island. Secured by tons of concrete, the two-and-a-quarter-mile bridge was the only connection between the mainland and the island. Buttressed by deep pilings, approved by the best engineers. No one questioned the Queen Isabella.

Until September 15, 2001. At two o'clock in the morning four barges and a tugboat crashed into the support system and brought the bridge down, plunging cars and people into the Laguna Madre eighty-five feet below. Eight people died when 240 feet of the bridge collapsed.[3]

You need never fear the same will happen to God's plan. His plan—born in eternity—will withstand any attack of humanity. Atheists, antagonists, skeptics, scholars—they've slammed into the bridge, but it has never budged. Texas engineers are regretting their work, but God will never regret his. "The Glory of Israel will not lie or have regret," declared Samuel, "for he is not a man, that he should have regret" (1 Samuel 15:29 ESV).

His plan—born in eternity—will withstand any attack of humanity.

God's plans will never change, because he makes his plans in complete knowledge. Forget hopeful forecasting. He declares "the end from the beginning" (Isaiah 46:10). Nothing takes him by surprise. "The plans of the LORD stand firm forever" (Psalm 33:11 NIV).

The cross will not lose its power. The blood of Christ will not fade in strength. Heaven will never announce the collapse of the bridge. God will never return to the drawing board. "What He does in time He planned from eternity. And all that He planned in eternity He carries out in time."[4]

"The LORD Almighty has spoken—who can change his plans? When his hand moves, who can stop him?" (Isaiah 14:27 NLT). God never changes. Everyone else does. Everything else will.

In the hours I prepared this message, the movers all but emptied the Lucado house. Christmas meals, dinner-table laughter, good-night hugs for my clan under that roof—all past tense. Yet another constant becomes a transient. What changes are you facing?

Cemeteries interrupt the finest families.

Retirement finds the best employees.

Age withers the strongest bodies.

With life comes change.

But with change comes the reassuring appreciation of heaven's permanence. His "firm foundation stands" (2 Timothy 2:19 ESV). His house will stand forever.

GOD'S GREAT LOVE

7

Several hundred feet beneath my chair is a lake, an underground cavern of crystalline water known as the Edwards Aquifer. We South Texans know much about this aquifer. We know its length (175 miles). We know its layout (west to east except under San Antonio, where it runs north to south). We know the water is pure. Fresh. It irrigates farms and waters lawns and fills pools and quenches thirst. We know much about the aquifer.

But for all the facts we do know, there is an essential one we don't. We don't know its size. The depth of the cavern? A mystery. Number of gallons? Unmeasured. No one knows the amount of water the aquifer contains.

Watch the nightly weather report, and you'd think otherwise. Meteorologists give regular updates on the aquifer level. You get the impression that the amount of water is calculated. "The truth is," a friend told me, "no one knows how much water is down there."

Could this be? I decided to find out. I called a water conservationist. "That's right," he affirmed. "We estimate. We try to measure. But the exact quantity? No one knows." Remarkable. We use it, depend upon it, would perish without it . . . but measure it? We can't.

Bring to mind another unmeasured pool? It might. Not a pool of water but a pool of love. God's love. Aquifer fresh. Pure as April snow. One swallow slackens the thirsty throat and softens the crusty heart. Immerse a life in God's love, and watch it emerge cleansed and changed. We know the impact of God's love.

But the volume? No person has ever measured it.

Moral meteorologists, worried we might exhaust the supply, suggest otherwise. "Don't drink too deeply," they caution, recommending rationed portions. Some people, after all, drink more than their share. Terrorists and traitors and wife beaters—let such scoundrels start drinking, and they may take too much.

But who has plumbed the depths of God's love? Only God has. "Want to see the size of my love?" he invites. "Ascend the winding path outside of Jerusalem. Follow the dots of

> GOD'S LOVE . . .
> ONE SWALLOW SLACKENS
> THE THIRSTY THROAT
> AND SOFTENS THE
> CRUSTY HEART.

bloody dirt until you crest the hill. Before looking up, pause and hear me whisper, 'This is how much I love you.'"

Whip-ripped muscles drape his back. Blood rivulets over his face. His eyes and lips are swollen shut. Pain rages at wildfire intensity. As he sinks to relieve the agony of his legs, his airway closes. At the edge of suffocation, he shoves pierced muscles against the spike and inches up the cross. He does this for hours. Painfully up and down until his strength and our doubts are gone.

Does God love you? Behold the cross, and behold your answer.

God the Son died for you. Who could have imagined such a gift? At the time Martin Luther was having his Bible printed in Germany, a printer's daughter encountered God's love. No one had told her about Jesus. Toward God she felt no emotion but fear. One day she gathered pieces of fallen Scripture from the floor. On one paper she found the words "For God so loved the world, that he gave . . . " The rest of the verse had not yet been printed. Still, what she saw was enough to move her. The thought that God would give anything moved her from fear to joy. Her mother noticed the change of attitude. When asked the cause of her happiness, the daughter produced the crumpled piece of partial verse from her pocket. The mother read it and asked, "What did he give?" The child was perplexed for a moment and then answered, "I do not know. But if He loved us well enough to give us anything, we should not be afraid of Him."[1]

Had God given his children a great idea or a lyrical message or an endless song . . . but he gave himself. "[God the Son] loved us and gave himself up for us as a fragrant offering and sacrifice to God" (Ephesians 5:2 NIV). What species of devotion is this? Find the answer under the category "unfailing." The holiness of God demanded a sinless sacrifice, and the only sinless sacrifice was God the Son. And since God's love never fails to pay the price, he did. God loves you with an unfailing love.

England saw a glimpse of such love in 1878. The second daughter of Queen Victoria was Princess Alice. Her young son was infected with a horrible affliction known as black diphtheria. Doctors quarantined the boy and told the mother to stay away.

But she couldn't. One day she overheard him whisper to the nurse, "Why doesn't my mother kiss me anymore?" The words melted her heart. She ran to her son and smothered him with kisses. Within a few days, she was buried.[2]

What would drive a mother to do such a thing? What would lead God to do something greater? Love. Trace the greatest action of God to the greatest attribute of God—his love.

But how does God's love square with the theme of this book? After all, "It's not about me." If it's not about me, does God care about me? God's priority is his glory. He occupies center stage; I carry props. He's the message; I'm but a word. Is this love?

No doubt. Do you really want the world to revolve around you? If it's all about you, then it's all up to you. Your Father rescues you from

IF IT'S ALL ABOUT YOU, THEN IT'S ALL UP TO YOU.

such a burden. While you are valuable, you aren't essential. You're important but not indispensable.

Still don't think that's good news?

Perhaps a story would be helpful. My father, an oil-field mechanic, never met a car he couldn't fix. Forget golf clubs or tennis rackets, my dad's toys were sockets and wrenches. He relished a wrecked engine. Once, while he was driving us to visit his sister in New Mexico, the car blew a rod. Most men would have groaned all the way to the mechanic. Not Dad. He called a tow truck and grinned the rest of the ride to my aunt's house. To this day I suspect paternal sabotage. A week of family chitchat repulsed him. But a week under the hood? *Forget the coffee and cookies. Hand me the manifold.* Dad did with a V-8 engine what Patton did with a platoon—he made it work.

Oh, that the same could be said for his youngest son. It can't. My problem with mechanics begins with the ends of the car. I can't remember which one holds the engine. Anyone who confuses the spare tire with the fan belt is likely not gifted in car repair.

My ignorance left my dad in a precarious position. What does a skilled mechanic do with a son who is anything but? As you begin formulating an answer, may I ask this question: What does God do with us? Under his care the universe runs like a Rolex. But his children? Most of us have trouble balancing a checkbook. So what does he do?

I know what my dad did. Much to his credit, he let me help him. He gave me jobs to do—holding wrenches, scrubbing spark plugs. And he knew my limits. Never once did he say, "Max, tear apart that transmission, will you? One of the gears is broken." Never said it. For one thing, he liked his transmission. For another, he loved me. He loved me too much to give me too much.

So does God. He knows your limitations. He's well aware of your weaknesses. You can no more die for your own sins than you can solve world hunger. And, according to him, that's okay. The world doesn't rely on you. God loves you too much to say it's all about you. He keeps the cosmos humming. You and I sprinkle sawdust on oil spots and thank him for the privilege. We've peeked under the hood. We don't know what it takes to run the world, and wise are we who leave the work to his hands.

To say "It's not about you" is not to say you aren't loved; quite the contrary. It's because God loves you that it's not about you.

And, oh, what a love this is. It's "too wonderful to be measured" (Ephesians 3:19 CEV). But though we cannot measure it, may I urge you to trust it? Some of you are so hungry for such love. Those who should have loved you didn't. Those who could have loved you wouldn't. You were left at the hospital. Left at the altar. Left with an empty bed. Left with a broken heart. Left with your question, "Does anybody love me?"

> YOU CAN NO MORE DIE FOR YOUR OWN SINS THAN YOU CAN SOLVE WORLD HUNGER.

Please listen to heaven's answer. As you ponder him on the cross, hear God assure, "I do."

Someday someone will likely find the limits of the South Texas aquifer. A robotic submarine, even a diver, will descend through the water until it hits solid ground. "We've plumbed the depths," newspapers will announce. Will someone say the same of God's love? No. When it comes to water, we'll find the limit. But when it comes to his love, we never will.

PART TWO

God-Promoting

CHAPTER EIGHT

GOD'S MIRRORS

8

G. R. Tweed looked across the Pacific waters at the American ship on the horizon. Brushing the jungle sweat from his eyes, the young naval officer swallowed deeply and made his decision. This could be his only chance for escape.

Tweed had been hiding on Guam for nearly three years. When the Japanese occupied the island in 1941, he ducked into the thick tropical brush. Survival hadn't been easy, but he preferred the swamp to a POW camp.

Late in the day July 10, 1944, he spotted the friendly vessel. He scurried up a hill and positioned himself on a cliff. Reaching into his pack, he pulled out a small mirror. At 6:20 P.M., he began sending signals. Holding the edge of the mirror in his fingers, he tilted it back and forth, bouncing the sunrays in the direction of the boat. Three short flashes. Three long. Three short again. Dot-dot-dot. Dash-dash-dash. Dot-dot-dot. SOS.

The signal caught the eye of a sailor on board the USS *McCall*. A rescue party boarded a motorized dinghy and slipped into the cove past the coastal guns. Tweed was rescued.[1]

He was glad to have that mirror, glad he knew how to use it, and glad that the mirror cooperated. Suppose it hadn't. (Prepare yourself for a crazy thought.) Suppose the mirror had resisted, pushed its own agenda. Rather than reflect a message from the sun, suppose it had opted to send its own. After all, three years of isolation would leave one starved for attention. Rather than sending an SOS, the mirror could have sent an LAM. "Look at me."

An egotistical mirror?

The only crazier thought would be an insecure mirror. *What if I blow it? What if I send a dash when I'm supposed to send a dot? Besides, have you seen the blemishes on my surface?* Self-doubt could paralyze a mirror.

So could self-pity. *Been crammed down in that pack, lugged through jungles, and now, all of a sudden expected to face the bright sun and perform a crucial service. No way. Staying in the pack. Not getting any reflection out of me.*

Good thing Tweed's mirror didn't have a mind of its own.

But God's mirrors? Unfortunately we do.

We are his mirrors, you know. Tools of heaven's heliography. Reduce the human job description down to one phrase, and this is it: Reflect God's glory. As Paul wrote: "And we, with our unveiled faces reflecting like mirrors the brightness of the Lord, all grow brighter and brighter as we are turned into the image that we reflect; this is the work of the Lord who is Spirit" (2 Corinthians 3:18 JB).

Some reader just arched an eyebrow. *Wait a second,* you are thinking. *I've read that passage before, more than once. And it sounded different.* Indeed it may have. Perhaps

REDUCE THE HUMAN JOB DESCRIPTION DOWN TO ONE PHRASE, AND THIS IS IT: REFLECT GOD'S GLORY.

it's because you are used to reading it in a different translation. "But we all, with unveiled face, *beholding as in a mirror* the glory of the Lord, are being transformed into the same image from glory to glory, just as from the Lord, the Spirit" (emphasis mine).

One translation says, "beholding as in a mirror;" another says, "reflecting like mirrors." One implies contemplation; the other implies refraction. Which is accurate?

Actually both. The verb *katoptrizo* can be translated either way. Translators are in both camps:

"with unveiled face, *beholding*" (RSV)

"*beholding* as in a glass" (KJV)

"*reflecting* like mirrors" (JB)

"be mirrors that brightly *reflect*" (TLB)

"we . . . all *reflect* the Lord's glory" (NIV)

But which meaning did Paul intend? In the context of the passage, Paul paralleled the Christian experience to the Mount Sinai experience of Moses. After the patriarch *beheld* the glory of God, his face *reflected* the glory of God. "The people of Israel could not bear to look at Moses' face. For his face shone with the glory of God" (2 Corinthians 3:7 NLT).

The face of Moses was so dazzling white that the "people of Israel could no more look right at him than stare into the sun" (2 Corinthians 3:7 MSG).

Upon beholding God, Moses could not help but reflect God. *The brightness he saw was the brightness he became.* Beholding led to becoming. Becoming led to reflecting. Perhaps the answer to the translation question, then, is "yes."

Did Paul mean "beholding as in a mirror"? Yes.

Did Paul mean "reflecting like a mirror"? Yes.

Could it be that the Holy Spirit intentionally selected a verb that would remind us to do both? To behold God so intently that we can't help but reflect him?

What does it mean to behold your face in a mirror? A quick glance? A casual look? No. To behold is to study, to stare, to contemplate. Beholding God's glory, then, is no side look or occasional glance; this beholding is a serious pondering.

Isn't that what we have done? We have camped at the foot of Mount Sinai and beheld the glory of God. Wisdom unsearchable. Purity unspotted. Years unending. Strength undaunted. Love immeasurable. Glimpses of the glory of God.

As we behold his glory, dare we pray that we, like Moses, will reflect it? Dare we hope to be mirrors in the hands of God, the reflection of the light of God? This is the call.

BEHOLDING LEADS TO BECOMING. BECOMING LEADS TO REFLECTING.

"Whatever you do, do all to the glory of God" (1 Corinthians 10:31 NKJV).

Whatever? Whatever.

Let your message reflect his glory. "Let your light shine before men, that they may see your good deeds and praise your Father in heaven" (Matthew 5:16 NIV).

Let your salvation reflect God's glory. "Having believed, you were marked in him with a seal, the promised Holy Spirit, who is a deposit guaranteeing our inheritance until the redemption of those who are God's possession—to the praise of his glory" (Ephesians 1:13–14 NIV).

Let your body reflect God's glory. "You are not your own.

. . . Glorify God in your body" (1 Corinthians 6:19–20).

Your struggles. "These sufferings of ours are for your benefit. And the more of you who are won to Christ, the more there are to thank him for his great kindness, and the more the Lord is glorified" (2 Corinthians 4:15 TLB; see also John 11:4).

Your success honors God. "Honor the LORD with your wealth" (Proverbs 3:9 NIV). "Riches and honor come from you" (1 Chronicles 29:12 NCV). "God . . . is giving you power to make wealth" (Deuteronomy 8:18).

Your message, your salvation, your body, your struggles, your success—all proclaim God's glory.

"Whatever you do in word or deed, do all in the name of the Lord Jesus, giving thanks through Him to God the Father" (Colossians 3:17).

HE SENDS THE MESSAGE; WE MIRROR IT.

He's the source; we are the glass. He's the light; we are the mirrors. He sends the message; we mirror it. We rest in his pack awaiting his call. And when placed in his hands, we do his work. It's not about us; it's all about him.

Mr. Tweed's use of a mirror led to a rescue.

May God's use of us lead to millions more.

My Message Is About Him

9

Behind him, a trail of tracks.

Beneath him, a pounding stallion.

Before him, miles of trail to cover.

Within him, a flint-rock resolve.

Squinty eyed. Firm jawed. Rawboned. Pony Express riders had one assignment—deliver the message safely and quickly. They seized every advantage: the shortest route, the fastest horse, the lightest saddle. Even the lightest lunchbox.

Only the sturdy were hired. Could they handle the horses? The heat? Could they outrun robbers and outlast blizzards? The young and the orphans were preferred. Those selected were given $125 a month (a good salary in 1860), a Colt revolver, a lightweight rifle, a bright red shirt, blue trousers, and eight hours to cover eighty miles, six days a week.

Hard work and high pay. But the message was worth it.[1]

The apostle Paul would have loved the Pony Express. For he, like the riders, had been entrusted with a message.

"I have a duty to all people," Paul told the Roman church (Romans 1:14 NCV). He had something for them—a message. He'd been entrusted as a Pony Express courier with a divine message, the gospel. Nothing mattered more to Paul than the gospel. "I am not ashamed of the gospel," he wrote next, "because it is the power of God for the salvation of everyone who believes" (Romans 1:16 NIV).

Paul existed to deliver the message. How people remembered him was secondary. (Else why would he introduce himself as a slave? Romans 1:1). How people remembered Christ was primary. Paul's message was not about himself. His message was all about Christ.

How difficult for us to maintain this focus. Don't we tend to tinker with the message? Aren't we prone to insert lines of self-service?

A young guide in the art museum was. One sentence summarized his job: Lead people to the paintings, answer their questions, and step out of the way. Initially he succeeded. He walked the clients to the framed treasures, identified the artists, and stepped out of view.

"This is a Monet," he would say and move back as people oohed and aahed and asked a question or two. When they were ready, he would lead them to the next masterpiece and repeat the sequence. "This is the work of Rembrandt." He stepped back; they leaned in. He stood; they stared.

Simple job. Delightful job. He took great pride in his work.

Too much pride, one might say. For in a short time, he forgot his role. He began thinking the people had come to see him. Rather than step away from the work of art, he lingered near it. As they oohed and aahed, he smiled. "Glad you like it," he replied, chest lifting, face blushing. He even responded with an occasional "thank you," taking credit for work he didn't do.

Visitors disregarded his comments. But they couldn't dismiss his movements. Lingering near a painting was no longer sufficient for the guide. Little by little he inched toward it. Initially extending his arm over the frame, then his torso over part of the canvas. Finally his body blocked the entire piece. People could see him but not the art. The very work he was sent to reveal he began to conceal.

That's when his Superior intervened. "This job isn't about you, Max. Don't obscure my masterpieces."

How many times has he had to remind me? The very first time I was called to display a painting, I was tempted to eclipse it.

The request came when I was twenty. "Can you address our church youth group?" We aren't talking citywide crusade here. Think more in terms of a dozen kids around a West Texas campfire. I was new to the faith, hence new to the power of the faith. I told my story, and, lo and behold, they listened! One even approached me afterward and said something like, "That moved me, Max." My chest lifted, and my feet shifted just a step in the direction of the painting.

God has been nudging me back ever since.

> I BELIEVE SATAN TRAINS BATTALIONS OF DEMONS TO WHISPER ONE QUESTION IN OUR EARS: "WHAT ARE PEOPLE THINKING OF YOU?"

Some of you don't relate. The limelight never woos you. You and John the Baptist sing the same tune: "He must become greater and greater, and I must become less and less" (John 3:30 NLT). God bless you. You might pray for the rest of us. We applause-aholics have done it all: dropped names, sung loudly, dressed up to look classy, dressed down to look cool, quoted authors we've never read, spouted Greek we've never studied. For the life of me, I believe Satan trains battalions of demons to whisper one question in our ears: "What are people thinking of you?"

A deadly query. What they think of us matters not. What they think of God matters all. God will not share his glory with another (Isaiah 42:8). Next time you need a nudge away from the spotlight, remember: *You are simply one link in a chain, an unimportant link at that.*

Don't agree? Take it up with the apostle. "So the one who plants *is not important*, and the one who waters *is not important*. Only God, who makes things grow, is important" (1 Corinthians 3:7 NCV, emphasis mine).

Remember the other messengers God has used?

A donkey to speak to Balaam (Numbers 22:28).

A staff-turned-snake to stir Pharaoh (Exodus 7:10).

He used stubborn oxen to make a point about reverence and a big fish to make a point about reluctant preachers (1 Samuel 6:1–12; Jonah 1:1–17).

God doesn't need you and me to do his work. We are expedient messengers, ambassadors by his kindness, not by our cleverness.

It's not about us, and it angers him when we think it is. Jesus has a stern warning for gallery guides who eclipse his work.

When you do something for someone else, don't call attention to yourself. You've seen them in action, I'm sure—"playactors" I call them—treating prayer meeting and street corner alike as a stage, acting compassionate as long as someone is watching, playing to the crowds. They get applause, true, but that's all they get. (Matthew 6:2 MSG)

Pony Express riders didn't take credit for kind letters. Gallery guides don't deserve applause for great art.

And we entrusted with the gospel dare not seek applause but best deflect applause. For our message is about Someone else.

> GOD DOESN'T NEED YOU AND ME TO DO HIS WORK. WE ARE EXPEDIENT MESSENGERS, AMBASSADORS BY HIS KINDNESS, NOT BY OUR CLEVERNESS.

A European village priest in medieval times once gathered his church for a special service. "Come tonight," he told them, "for a special sermon on Jesus." And they did. They came. To their surprise, however, no candles illuminated the sanctuary. They groped their way to the pews and took their seats. The priest was nowhere to be seen. But soon he was heard walking through the church toward the front. When he reached the crucifix that hung on the wall, he lit a candle. Saying nothing, he illuminated the pierced feet of Christ, then the side, then one hand, and then the other. Lifting the candle, he shed light on the blood-masked face and the crown of thorns. With a puff, he blew out the candle and dismissed the church.[2]

May we do nothing more.

May we do nothing less.

MY SALVATION
IS ABOUT HIM

10

A large American food company released the perfect cake mix. It required no additives. No eggs, no sugar. Just mix some water with the powder, pop the pan in the oven, and presto! Prepare yourself for a treat.

One problem surfaced. No one purchased the product! Puzzled, the manufacturer conducted surveys, identified the reason, and reissued the cake with a slight alteration. The instructions now called for the cook to add one egg. Sales sky-rocketed.[1]

Why are we like that? What makes us want to add to what is already complete? Paul asked the same questions. People puzzled him by adding their work to a finished project. Not eggs to a recipe but requirements for salvation. Not much, just one small rule: You must be circumcised to be saved.

Such talk rankled the apostle. "We . . . put no confidence in the flesh," he declared (Philippians 3:3 NIV). "God's way of making us right with himself depends on faith—counting on

Christ alone" (3:9 TLB, emphasis mine). Paul proclaimed a pure grace: no mixtures, no additives, no alterations. The work of Christ is the bungee cord for the soul. Trust it and take the plunge.

We quickly side with Paul on the circumcision controversy. The whole discussion sounds odd to our Western ears. But is it so strange? We may not teach Jesus + circumcision, but how about:

Jesus + evangelism: *How many people have you led to Christ this year?* Or:

Jesus + contribution: *Are you giving all you can to the church?* Or:

Jesus + mysticism: *You do offer penance and pray to the Virgin Mary, don't you?* Or:

Jesus + heritage: *Were you raised in "the church"?* Or:

Jesus + doctrine: *When you were baptized, was the water running or still? Deep or shallow? Hot or cold?*

Legalism. The theology of "Jesus +." Legalists don't dismiss Christ. They trust in Christ a lot. But they don't trust in Christ alone.

We're tempted to dismiss legalism as harmless. After all, legalists look good. They act religious. They promote morality and decency and good living. Is there any harm to their teaching?

Paul responds with a resounding "yes!" He reserves a biting

tone for the legalist. "Watch out for those who do evil, who are like dogs, who demand to cut the body" (Philippians 3:2 NCV). Ouch! Can you hear the intolerance in those terms? "Evil." "Dogs." Those "who demand to cut the body" or, as one paraphrase renders it, "knife-happy circumcisers" (MSG).

Why the bared fangs? Why the hot ink? Paul didn't go barefisted with others this way. Though antiadultery, he didn't call two-timers names. He was

> LEGALISTS TRUST IN CHRIST A LOT. BUT THEY DON'T TRUST IN CHRIST ALONE.

intolerant of homosexuality, but he didn't blast the gay crowd with a verbal blowtorch. He preached against drunkenness, but did he ever call drunks "dogs"?

And if you think he's ticked off in this passage, read his wish for the legalists of Galatia. "I wish the people who are bothering you would castrate themselves" (Galatians 5:12 NCV).

Why the intensity? Why so strident against legalists? Simple. Self-salvation makes light of our problem.

On our own, we're spiritually sunk, my friend. As sunk as the *Kursk*. Remember the nuclear submarine *Kursk*, the pride of the Russian navy? August 12, 2000, was to be her banner day. Five high-ranking naval officers journeyed to sea to witness a demonstration of her strength. But then came two explosions, enormous thundering booms that registered 1.5 and 3.5 on the Richter scale. Something had gone dreadfully wrong.

The seven-ton vessel immediately took on water and plunged 350 feet to the seabed of the Arctic Ocean. Most of the 118 crew members died instantly. Others were left to spend their last hours in freezing, horrid conditions.[2]

Are we not like the sailors? Are we not equally helpless and hopeless? Like them, we are submerged—not in salt water but in sin. We need to be lifted up—not out of the ocean but out of our failures. "There is no one who always does what is right, not even one" (Romans 3:10 NCV). Like the sailors, we've hit bottom.

But suppose one of the submerged sailors thought of a solution. Suppose he declared to his fellow crewmen, "I know what to do. Let's all press our hands on the ceiling and push. We will shove the sub to the surface." Can you imagine the looks the crew would give him? *Push a seven-ton vessel up through 350 feet of water?* If they said anything, they would tell him to come to his senses. "You don't understand the gravity of the situation. We don't have what it takes to save our lives. We aren't strong enough. We aren't big enough. We don't need muscles; we need a miracle."

Paul's point precisely. Separating you and God is not 350

feet of ocean water but an insurmountable flood of imperfection and sin. Do you think that by virtue of your moral muscle you can push this vessel to the surface? Do you think your baptism and Sunday attendance will be enough to save you?

Legalists do. They miss the gravity of the problem. By offering to help, they not only make light of sin, they mock God.

Who would look at the cross of Christ and say, "Great work, Jesus. Sorry you couldn't finish it, but I'll take up the slack"?

> LEGALISM IS JOYLESS
> BECAUSE LEGALISM IS
> ENDLESS.

Dare we question the crowning work of God? Dare we think heaven needs our help in saving us? We're stuck on the bottom of the ocean. We can't see the light of day! Legalism discounts God and in the process makes a mess out of us.

To anyone attempting to earn heaven, Paul asks, "How is it that you are turning back to those weak and miserable principles? Do you wish to be enslaved by them all over again? . . . What has happened to all your joy?" (Galatians 4:9, 15 NIV).

Legalism is joyless because legalism is endless. There is always another class to attend, person to teach, mouth to feed. Inmates incarcerated in self-salvation find work but never joy.

How could they? They never know when they are finished. Legalism leaches joy.

Grace, however, dispenses peace. The Christian trusts a finished work. "Gone are the exertions of law-keeping, gone the disciplines and asceticism of legalism, gone the anxiety that having done everything we might not have done enough. We reach the goal not by the stairs, but by the lift. . . . God pledges his promised righteousness to those who will stop trying to save themselves."[3]

Grace offers rest. Legalism never does. Then why do we embrace it? "Those who trust in themselves are foolish" (Proverbs 28:26 NCV). Why do we trust in ourselves? Why do we add to God's finished work? Might the answer include the verb *boast?*

Saving yourself is heady stuff. Even headier than a high school varsity football jacket. I still own mine. I wore it every day of my senior year. Who cared if the temperature was in the nineties? I wanted everyone to see what I had accomplished. If making a football team feels great, how much more would earning a spot on God's team?

But the truth is, we don't. If we think we do, we have missed the message. "What is left for us to brag about?" Paul wonders (Romans 3:27 CEV). What is there indeed? What have you contributed? Aside from your admission of utter decadence, I can't think of a thing. "By His doing you are in Christ Jesus" (1 Corinthians 1:30). Salvation glorifies the Savior, not the saved.

Your salvation showcases God's mercy. It makes nothing of your effort but everything of his. "I—yes, I alone—am the one who blots out your sins *for my own sake* and will never think of them again" (Isaiah 43:25 NLT, emphasis mine). He saves us for the same reason he saved the Jews:

> For my own sake and for the honor of my name I will hold back my anger and not wipe you out. I refined you in the furnace of affliction, but found no silver there. You are worthless, with nothing good in you at all. Yet for my own sake—yes, *for my own sake*—I will save you from my anger and not destroy you lest the heathen say their gods have conquered me. I will not let them have my glory (Isaiah 48:9–11 TLB).

Can you add anything to this salvation? No. The work is finished.

YOUR SALVATION SHOWCASES GOD'S MERCY. IT MAKES NOTHING OF YOUR EFFORT BUT EVERYTHING OF HIS.

Can you earn this salvation? No. Don't dishonor God by trying.

Dare we boast about this salvation? By no means. The giver of bread, not the beggar, deserves praise. "Let him who boasts, boast in the Lord" (1 Corinthians 1:31).

It's not about what we do; it's all about what he does.

My Body Is About Him

11

You're acquainted with house-sitters. You've possibly used one. Not wanting to leave your house vacant, you ask someone to stay in your home until you return. Let me describe two of your nightmares.

The house-sitter redecorates your house. White paint is changed to pink. Berber carpet to shag. An abstract plastic chair sits in the place of your cozy love seat. His justification? "The house didn't express me accurately. I needed a house that communicated who I am."

Your response? "It's not yours! My residence does not exist to reflect you! I asked you to take care of the house, not take over the house!" Would you want a sitter like this?

You might choose him over nightmare number two. She didn't redecorate; she neglected. Never washed a dish, made a bed, or took out the trash. "My time here was temporary. I knew you wouldn't mind," she explains.

Of course you'd mind! Does she know what this abode cost you?

Both house-sitters made the same mistake. They acted as if the dwelling were theirs. How could they?

Or, better asked, how could we? When it comes to our bodies, the Bible declares that we don't own them. "You are no longer your own. God paid a great price for you. So use your body to honor God" (1 Corinthians 6:19–20 CEV).

Use your body to indulge your passions? To grab attention? To express your opinions? No. Use your body to honor God. "Use your whole body as a tool to do what is right for the glory of God" (Romans 6:13 NLT). Your body is God's instrument, intended for his work and for his glory.

The Corinthian Christians had serious trouble with this. When it came to the body, they insisted, "We can do anything we want to" (1 Corinthians 6:12 CEV). Their philosophy conveniently separated flesh from spirit. Have fun with the flesh. Honor God with the spirit. Wild Saturdays. Worshipful Sundays. You can have it all.

Paul disagreed. He dismissed the dichotomy. He reminded his readers that God interwove body with soul, elevating them to equal status. Your body is no toy. Quite the contrary. Your body is a tool. "Do you not know that your bodies are members of Christ himself?" (1 Corinthians 6:15 NIV).

I remember seeing a sign on a mechanic's toolbox that read: "Don't ask to borrow my tools. I use them to feed my family." Understandable request. To do his work, the mechanic needed his instruments. He needed them present and functional. When he looked for his wrench, he wanted to find it. When he pulled out a screwdriver, he wanted it to be clean. His work was important; hence his tools were important.

What work is more important than God's? Doesn't it stand to reason that God's tools should be maintained?

Hold on there. I heard that sigh. *Maintain my body? I don't want to talk about my body.*

We've heard it all, haven't we? Eat balanced meals. Exercise regularly. Avoid fat. Eat

YOUR BODY IS GOD'S INSTRUMENT, INTENDED FOR HIS WORK AND FOR HIS GLORY.

protein. Get rest. We've heard it all. And we've blown it all. Each of us has. To one degree or another we have mismanaged our bodies. You're thinking, *Lucado is reaching for the guilt hammer.* I'm not. You don't need a reprimand. A reminder maybe, but a reprimand? No. Yes, your belly may be a bit soft, but so is your heart. Soft for Christ. Soft for others. Otherwise you wouldn't be reading this book. Stay that way. "Workouts in the gymnasium are useful, but a disciplined life in God is far more so, making you fit both today and forever" (1 Timothy 4:8 MSG). If forced to choose, take the soft heart over the hard body.

But I don't think a choice is required. Maintain God's instrument. Feed it. Rest it. When he needs a sturdy implement—a servant who is rested enough to serve, fueled enough to work, alert enough to think—let him find one in you. He uses you.

Greater still, he lives in you. "Don't you know that your body is the temple of the Holy Spirit, who lives in you?" (1 Corinthians 6:19 NLT). Paul wrote these words to counter the Corinthian sex obsession. "Run away from sexual sin!" reads the prior sentence. "No other sin so clearly affects the body as this one does. For sexual immorality is a sin against your own body" (v. 18 NLT).

What a salmon scripture! No message swims more upstream than this one. You know the sexual anthem of our day: "I'll do what I want. It's my body." God's firm response? "No, it's not. It's mine."

Be quick to understand, God is not antisex. Dismiss any notion that God is antiaffection and anti-intercourse. After all, he developed the whole package. Sex was his idea. From his perspective, sex is nothing short of holy.

He views sexual intimacy the way I view our family Bible. Passed down from my father's side, the volume is one hundred years old and twelve inches thick. Replete with lithographs, scribblings, and a family tree, it is, in my estimation, beyond value. Hence, I use it carefully.

When I need a stepstool, I don't reach for the Bible. If the foot of my bed breaks, I don't use the family Bible as a prop. When we need old paper for wrapping, we don't rip a sheet out of this book. We reserve the heirloom for special times and keep it in a chosen place.

Regard sex the same way—as a holy gift to be opened in a special place at special times. The special place is marriage, and the time is with your spouse.

Casual sex, intimacy outside of marriage, pulls the Corinthian ploy. It pretends we can give the body and not affect the soul. We can't. We humans are so intricately psychosomatic that whatever touches the *soma* impacts the *psyche* as well. The me-centered phrase "as long as no one gets hurt" sounds noble, but the truth is, we don't know who gets hurt. God-centered thinking rescues us from the sex we thought would make us happy. You may think your dalliances are harmless, and years may pass before the x-rays reveal the internal damage, but don't be fooled. Casual sex is a diet of chocolate—it tastes good for a while, but the imbalance can ruin you. Sex apart from God's plan wounds the soul.

Sex according to God's plan nourishes the soul. Consider his plan. Two children of God make a covenant with each other. They disable the ejection seats. They burn the bridge back to Momma's house. They fall into each other's arms beneath the canopy of God's blessing, encircled by the tall fence of fidelity. Both know the other will be there in the morning. Both know the other will stay even as skin wrinkles and vigor fades. Each gives the other exclusive for-your-eyes-only privileges. Gone is the guilt. Gone the undisciplined lust. What remains is a celebration of permanence, a tender moment in which the body continues what the mind and the soul have already begun. A time in which "the man and his wife were both naked and were not ashamed" (Genesis 2:25).

Such sex honors God. And such sex satisfies God's children. Several years ago *USA Today* ran an article with this lead:

Aha, call it the revenge of the church ladies. Sigmund Freud said they suffer from an "obses-

> SEX IS A CELEBRATION OF PERMANENCE, A TENDER MOMENT IN WHICH THE BODY CONTINUES WHAT THE MIND AND THE SOUL HAVE ALREADY BEGUN.

sional neurosis" accompanied by guilt, suppressed emotions and repressed sexuality. Former *Saturday Night Live* comedian Dana Carvey satirized them as uptight prudes who believe sex is downright dirty. But several major research studies show that church ladies (and the men who sleep with them) are among the most sexually satisfied people on the face of the earth. Researchers at the University of Chicago seem to think so. Several years ago when they released the results of the most "comprehensive and methodologically sound" sex survey ever conducted, they reported that religious women experienced significantly higher levels of sexual satisfaction than non-religious women.[1]

(I'm thinking this article would be an effective evangelism tool.)

Your body, God's tool. Maintain it.

Your body, God's temple. Respect it.

"God owns the whole works. So let people see God in and through your body" (1 Corinthians 6:20 MSG).

Manage God's house in such a way that passersby stop and notice. "Who lives in that house?" they will ask. And when they hear the answer, God will be honored.

MY STRUGGLES
ARE ABOUT HIM

12

Martin and Gracia Burnham married with mission work in their hearts.[1] For seventeen years they served God in the Philippines. With three children born on the mission field and valuable skills in the ministry's aviation program, they were acclimated and essential to the work. He, single-minded. She, gracious and convicted.

Then why didn't God block the bullets? Why did he let her get shot? And why did God let him die?

On May 27, 2001, while celebrating their eighteenth wedding anniversary at a beachside resort, Martin and Gracia were taken hostage by a militant terrorist organization with ties to Osama bin Laden. Captors chained the couple to guards, marched them through jungles, and rationed their food. They endured seventeen firefights and for over four hundred days were either running for their lives or bored. Their health deteriorated, but their faith remained sturdy. "We might not leave this jungle alive," said Martin, "but at least we can leave this world serving the Lord with gladness." A premonition led Martin to write a farewell letter to his children.

The premonition proved accurate. On June 7, 2002, Philippine Rangers attacked the terrorist camp, catching Martin and Gracia in the cross-fire. One bullet entered her leg. Another took his life. She was left a widow, and we are left to wonder why. Is this how God honors his chosen? How do you explain such a tragedy?

And as you're thinking of theirs, how do you explain yours? The tension at home. The demands at work. The bills on your desk or the tumor in your body. You aren't taken hostage, but aren't you occasionally taken aback by God's silence? He knows what you are facing. How do we explain this?

Maybe God messed up. Cancer cells crept into your DNA when he wasn't looking. He was so occupied with the tornado in Kansas that he forgot the famine in Uganda. He tried to change the stubborn streak in your spouse but just couldn't get him to budge. Honestly. A bumbling Creator? An absent-minded Maker? What evidence does Scripture provide to support such a view? What evidence does creation offer? Can't the Maker of heaven and earth handle bad traffic and prevent bad marriages? Of course he can. Then why doesn't he?

Perhaps he is mad. Have we so exhausted the mercy of God's bank account that every prayer bounces like a bad check? Did humanity cross the line millenniums ago, and now we're getting what we deserve? Such an argument carries a dash of merit. God does leave us to the consequences of our stupid decisions. Think Egyptian soldiers in Red Sea, Hebrews in Babylon, Peter weeping with the sound of a crowing rooster in his ears. Bang your head against the wall, and expect a headache. God lets us endure the fruit of sin. But to label him peeved and impatient? To do so you need to scissor from your Bible some tender passages such as:

> GOD is sheer mercy and grace;
>> not easily angered, he's rich in love.
> He doesn't endlessly nag and scold,
>> nor hold grudges forever.
> He doesn't treat us as our sins deserve,
>> nor pay us back in full for our wrongs.
> As high as heaven is over the earth,
>> so strong is his love to those who fear him.
> (Psalm 103:8–11 MSG)

Don't blame suffering in the world on the anger of God. He's not mad; he didn't mess up. Follow our troubles to their headwaters, and you won't find an angry or befuddled God. But you will find a sovereign God.

Your pain has a purpose. Your problems, struggles, heartaches, and hassles cooperate toward one end—the glory of God. "Trust me in your times of trouble, and I will rescue you, and you will give me glory" (Psalm 50:15 NLT).

Not an easy assignment to swallow. Not for you. Not for me. Not for the blind man on the side of the road. When Jesus and his followers passed him, the disciples had a question.

> As He [Jesus] passed by, He saw a man blind from birth. And His disciples asked Him, "Rabbi, who sinned, this man or his parents, that he would be born blind?" Jesus answered, "It was neither that this man sinned, nor his parents; but it was so that the works of God might be displayed in him." (John 9:1–3)

> YOUR PAIN HAS A PURPOSE. YOUR PROBLEMS, STRUGGLES, HEARTACHES, AND HASSLES COOPERATE TOWARD ONE END—THE GLORY OF GOD.

Born blind. A lifetime of darkness. Never saw a mother smile or a sunset fade. *Who did this?* the disciples wondered, anxious to blame someone. Such a bad plight can be traced back to a bad deed. Right?

Wrong, Jesus replied. Don't search the family tree. Don't

request a copy of the man's rap sheet. Blame this blindness on a call from God. Why was the man sightless? So "the works of God might be displayed in him."

Odds are, he would have preferred another role in the human drama. Compared to others, his assignment held little glamour.

"Mary, be a mother to my son."

"Peter, you'll be my first preacher."

"Matthew, the first gospel? It's all yours."

Then God turns to this man, "And you?"

"Yes, Lord?"

"You'll be blind for my glory."

"I'll be blind?"

"Yes."

"For your glory?"

"Yes."

"But I don't understand."

"You'll see."

The blind man wasn't the only candidate for a complaint. Consider the case of Martha and Mary. Personal friends of Jesus. Confidantes. He stayed at their house and ate at their table. And when their brother, Lazarus, became ill, the sisters blitzed a message to Jesus. If the Nazarene would heal anyone, it would be Lazarus.

Wrong again. "But when Jesus heard this, He said, 'This sickness is not to end in death, but for the glory of God, so that the Son of God may be glorified by it'" (John 11:4).

Feverish, clammy, knocking on the door of death—why? Because he ate the wrong food? Didn't guard his health? Drank too much? None of these. He was sick for the sake of God. Call it the assignment of sickness. How else do you explain the puzzle of the next two verses?

"Now Jesus loved Martha and her sister and Lazarus. So when He heard that he was sick, He then stayed two days longer in the place where He was" (John 11:5–6).

Talk about a left turn. You'd expect the verse to read: "Jesus loved Martha and her sister and Lazarus . . . so he made a fast dash to their house to heal Lazarus." Just the opposite occurred. Because Jesus loved the trio, he lingered until Lazarus died.

Blindness displays the works of Christ? Death glorifies the power of Christ? How can this be?

I'm looking around my office for an answer. A frame displays my favorite picture of Denalyn. A metal stand displays an antique pot. My brother gave me a stained-glass window from a country church. It is displayed by virtue of two wires and two hooks. Picture frames and metal stands, wires and hooks— different tools, same job. They display treasures.

What these do for artifacts, the blind man did for Christ.

He was the frame in which Jesus' power was seen, the stand upon which Jesus' miracle was placed. Born sightless to display heaven's strength. Do you suppose the sight of his sight showcased the work of Christ?

IS THERE ANY CHANCE, ANY POSSIBILITY, THAT YOU HAVE BEEN SELECTED TO STRUGGLE FOR GOD'S GLORY?

And the fading pulse and final breath of Lazarus? You think the news of a three-days-dead man walking out of a tomb amplified God's power?

And you? Now it gets a bit sticky. What about your struggles? Is there any chance, any possibility, that you have been selected to struggle for God's glory? Have you "been granted for Christ's sake, not only to believe in Him, but also to suffer for His sake" (Philippians 1:29)?

Here is a clue. Do your prayers seem to be unanswered? What you request and what you receive aren't matching up? Don't think God is not listening. Indeed he is. He may have higher plans.

Here is another. Are people strengthened by your struggles? A friend of mine can answer yes. His cancer was consuming more than his body; it was eating away at his faith. Unanswered petitions perplexed him. Well-meaning Christians confused him. "If you have faith," they said, "you will be healed."

No healing came. Just more chemo, nausea, and questions. He assumed the fault was a small faith. I suggested another answer. "It's not about you," I told him. "Your hospital room is a showcase for your Maker. Your faith in the face of suffering cranks up the volume of God's song."

Oh, that you could have seen the relief on his face. To know that he hadn't failed God and God hadn't failed him— this made all the difference. Seeing his sickness in the scope of God's sovereign plan gave his condition a sense of dignity. He accepted his cancer as an assignment from heaven: a missionary to the cancer ward. A week later I saw him again. "I reflected God," he said, smiling through a thin face, "to the nurses, the doctors, my friends. Who knows who needed to see God, but I did my best to make him seen."

Bingo. His cancer paraded the power of Jesus down the Main Street of his world. He, the blind man, Lazarus, and millions of others form a unique society: selected to suffer for God's glory. His light prisms through their aching lives and spills forth in a cascade of colors. God-glimpses.

God will use whatever he wants to display his glory. Heavens and stars. History and nations. People and problems. A kidnapped couple in the Philippines. My dying dad in West Texas.

The last three years of his life were scarred by ALS. The disease took him from a healthy mechanic to a bedbound paralytic. He lost his voice and his muscles, but he never lost his faith. Visitors noticed. Not so much in what he said but more in what he didn't say. Never outwardly angry or bitter, Jack Lucado suffered stately.

His faith led one man to seek a like faith. After the funeral this man sought me out and told me. Because of my dad's example, he became a Jesus follower.

> YOUR FAITH IN THE FACE OF SUFFERING CRANKS UP THE VOLUME OF GOD'S SONG.

Did God orchestrate my father's illness for that very reason? Knowing the value he places on one soul, I wouldn't be surprised. And imagining the splendor of heaven, I know my father's not complaining.

A season of suffering is a small assignment when compared to the reward.

Rather than begrudge your problem, explore it. Ponder it. And most of all, use it. Use it to the glory of God.

Martin and Gracia did.

During their captivity, they not only spoke of Jesus, they

lived Jesus. Didn't complain. Did their work and volunteered for more. Chained every night to a guard, Martin always wished his captors a good night and told them about Jesus. The Burnhams allowed God to use their suffering for his glory.

Because of Martin's death, nations around the world heard the name of Christ. I heard the report on a London, England, news channel. Millions saw the forbearing figure of his wife and heard a moving interview with his father, who said God would get them through this. Every major network gave priceless minutes to the story of a man who loved Christ more than life.

Through the Burnhams' struggle, God was seen.

Through Martin's death, God was seen.

Through your problems and mine, may he be seen as well.

My Success
Is About Him

13

How well do you know the following people and organizations?

Jack Tinker and Partners

Doyle Dane Bernbach

BBDO

Foote, Cone and Belding

J. Walter Thompson

How did you do? Not too good? If not, then the ones on the list are pleased. Advertising agencies don't exist to make a name for themselves. They exist to make a name for others. While you may not be acquainted with the companies, aren't you familiar with their work?

"Plop, plop, fizz, fizz, oh what a relief it is." The work of Jack Tinker and Partners for Alka-Seltzer in 1976.

"We try harder." Doyle Dane Bernbach created the slogan for Avis Rent A Car in 1962.

"M'm! M'm! Good! M'm! M'm! Good!" Credit BBDO with the catch-phrase Campbell's Soup has used since 1935.

While you've never heard of Foote, Cone and Belding, have you ever heard this motto: "When you care enough to send the very best"? Hallmark began using the line in 1934.

You don't hum the name of J. Walter Thompson, but have you hummed the jingle his agency wrote for Kellogg's "Snap! Crackle! Pop!" Rice Krispies?[1]

We could learn a lesson from these companies. What they do for clients, we exist to do for Christ. To live "reflecting like mirrors the brightness of the Lord" (2 Corinthians 3:18 JB).

As heaven's advertising agency, we promote God in every area of life, including success.

That's right—even your success is intended to reflect God. Listen to the reminder Moses gave the children of Israel: "Always remember that it is the LORD your God who gives you power to become rich, and he does it to fulfill the covenant he made with your ancestors" (Deuteronomy 8:18 NLT).

From where does success come? God. "It is the LORD your God who gives you power to become rich."

And why does he give it? For his reputation. "To fulfill the covenant he made with your ancestors."

God blessed Israel in order to billboard his faithfulness. When foreigners saw the fruitful farms of the Promised Land, God did not want them to think about the farmer but the farmer's Maker. Their success advertised God.

Nothing has changed. God lets you excel so you can make him known. And you can be sure of one thing: God will make you good at something. This is his principle: "True humility and fear of the LORD lead to riches, honor, and long life" (Proverbs 22:4 NLT).

Would we expect any less? A godly life often results in success. Consider a construction worker, for example. Imagine a trouble-making, hard-drinking fellow. Before he knows Christ, he's not much of an employee. Frequent hangovers, padded expense accounts. Sneaks out early on Friday afternoons . . . He does it all. And he pays the price —overdue bills, bail-bond debts, a resumé that reads like a rap sheet.

GOD LETS YOU EXCEL SO YOU CAN MAKE HIM KNOWN.

But then Christ finds him. Not only does God save his soul, he straightens out the man's work habits. The guy shows up on time. He does his job. He stops complaining and starts volunteering. Everything improves—attitude, productivity, cooperation.

And guess who notices? His boss. And guess what happens? Promotions. Pay increases. The company truck and credit card. Success. But with the success comes a problem.

Just ask Nadab, Elah, and Omri. Or interview Ahab, Ahaziah, or Jehoram. Ask these men to describe the problem of success. *I would*, you might be thinking, *if I knew who they were.* My point exactly. These are men we should know. They were kings of Israel. They ascended to the throne ... but something about the throne brought them down. Their legacies are stained with blood spilling and idol worship. They failed at success. They forgot both the source and purpose of their success. King Nadab symbolized them all: "He did evil in the sight of the LORD, and walked in the way of his father and in his sin which he made Israel sin" (1 Kings 15:26).

You won't be offered a throne, but you might be offered a corner office, a scholarship, an award, a new contract, a pay raise. You won't be given a kingdom to oversee, but you might be given a home or employees or students or money or resources. You will, to one degree or another, succeed.

And when you do, you might be tempted to forget who helped you do so. Success sabotages the memories of the successful. Kings of the mountain forget who carried them up the trail.

The flea did. An old fable tells of an elephant lumbering across a wooden bridge suspended over a ravine. As the big animal crossed over the worn-out structure, it creaked and groaned under the elephant's weight. When he reached the

other side, a flea that had nestled itself in the elephant's ear proclaimed, "Boy, did we shake that bridge!"[2]

The flea had done nothing! The elephant had done all the
work.

What a fleabrained dec-
laration! But don't we do
the same? The man who
begged for help in medical
school ten years ago is too
busy to worship today. Back
when the family struggled
to make ends meet, they
leaned on God for daily
bread. Now that there is an

> SUCCESS SABOTAGES
> THE MEMORIES OF THE
> SUCCESSFUL. KINGS OF
> THE MOUNTAIN FORGET
> WHO CARRIED THEM
> UP THE TRAIL.

extra car in the garage and a jingle in the pocket, they haven't
spoken to him in a while. In the early days of the church, the
founding members spent hours in prayer. Today the church is
large, well attended, well funded. Who needs to pray?

Success begets amnesia. Doesn't have to, however. God
offers spiritual ginseng to help your memory. His prescription
is simply "Know the purpose of success." Why did God help
you succeed? So you can make him known.

David Robinson knows this. Speaking of someone who
God made good, this seven-foot-tall basketball player for the

San Antonio Spurs was good. For fourteen seasons he dominated the league: MVP, All-Star, two championship rings, two Olympic gold medals. But it was his character that caught the attention of the public. These words appeared in the *Washington Times* the day after Robinson's departing championship victory.

> Robinson showed that a player did not have to be cheap or dirty to be effective. He did not have to clutter his body with tattoos or litter the NBA cities with illegitimate children. Robinson never felt a need to bring attention to himself, to shimmy after a good play or point to the crowd, as if to say, "Look at me. Aren't I something special?"
>
> The good guys won. Robinson won. Decency won. We all won.[3]

Minutes after hoisting the trophy overhead, David was interviewed by a national network. "People in San Antonio know what I'm going to say," he told the reporter. And we did. We did because we had heard him say it and seen him live it for so long. "All the glory goes to God," he announced.

Three thousand years ago another David declared the same truth. "Riches and honor come from you alone, for you rule over everything. Power and might are in your hand, and it is at your discretion that people are made great and given strength" (1 Chronicles 29:12 NLT).

"They did not conquer the land with their swords; it was not their own strength that gave them victory. It was by your mighty power that they succeeded; it was because you favored them and smiled on them" (Psalm 44:3 NLT).

I know a frog who needed those verses. He had a real problem. His home pond was drying up. If he didn't find water soon, he would do the same. Word reached him of a vibrant stream over the adjacent hill. If only he could live there. But how could he? The short legs of a frog were not made for long journeys.

But then he had an idea. Convincing two birds to carry either end of a stick, he bit the center and held on as they flew. As they winged toward the new water, his jaws clamped tightly. It was quite a sight! Two birds, one stick, and a frog in the middle. Down below, a cow in a pasture saw them passing overhead. Impressed, he wondered aloud, "Now who came up with that idea?"

IT'S ALL ABOUT HIM—
HIS PRESENT AND
FUTURE GLORY.

The frog overheard his question and couldn't resist a reply. "I diiiiiiii . . ."

Don't make the same mistake. "Pride goes before destruction, and haughtiness before a fall" (Proverbs 16:18 NLT). Why are you good at what you do? For your comfort? For your retirement? For your self-esteem? No. Deem these as bonuses, not as the reason. Why are you good at what you do? For God's sake. Your success is not about what you do. It's all about him—his present and future glory.

UPWARD THINKING

14

"So, you like Jewish authors?"

The fellow asking the question sat on the aisle seat. I had the window, which meant I had a view of the runway. The mechanical crew was repairing a bird dent on the wing. While they worked, I read. As I read my Bible, the rabbi interrupted.

"So, you like Jewish authors?"

The twinkle in his eye betrayed his pleasure in the question. His chest-length mop of a beard couldn't hide his smile. I had spotted him earlier in the waiting area. The tassels from his shirttail and hair-clipped yarmulke led me to peg him as the pious, silent type.

Pious. Yes. But silent? He loved to talk. He loved to talk Torah. I was in for a lesson. Tucked away in the ceremonies and laws of Moses, he explained, are pictures of God. Who could offer a sacrifice and not weep for God's grace? Who could read about servants redeeming their kinsmen and not think about

God redeeming us? And who could read the third command-ment without remembering to live for God's glory?

I signaled a time-out, opened to Exodus, and read the third command: "You shall not take the name of the LORD your God in vain" (20:7). My puzzled expression was enough to request an explanation.

"Don't think language; think lifestyle," he instructed. "The command calls us to elevate the name or reputation of God to the highest place. We exist to give honor to his name. May I illustrate?"

> WE EXIST TO GIVE HONOR TO HIS NAME.

By now the damaged wing was fixed (the plane's; can't speak for the bird). And as we gained altitude, so did the rabbi. I took notes. He proceeded to create a story involving a Man-hattan skyscraper. Everyone in the building works for the CEO, who offices on the top floor. Most have not seen him, but they have seen his daughter. She works in the building for her father. She exploits her family position to her benefit.

One morning she approaches Bert, the guard. "I'm hungry, Bert. Go down the street and buy me a Danish."

The demand places Bert in a quandary. He's on duty.

Leaving his post puts the building at risk. But his boss's daughter insists, "Come on, now; hurry up."

What option does he have? As he leaves, he says nothing but thinks something like, *If the daughter is so bossy, what does that say about her father?*

She's only getting started. Munching on her muffin, she bumps into a paper-laden secretary. "Where are you going with all those papers?"

"To have them bound for an afternoon meeting."

"Forget the meeting. Come to my office and vacuum the carpet."

"But I was told . . ."

"And I am telling you something else."

The woman has no choice. After all, this is the boss's daughter speaking. Which causes the secretary to question the wisdom of the boss.

And on the daughter goes. Making demands. Calling shots. Interrupting schedules. Never invoking the name of her dad. Never leveraging her comments with, "My dad said . . ."

No need to.

Isn't she the boss's child? Doesn't the child speak for the father? And so Bert abandons his post. An assistant fails to finish a task. And more than one employee questions the wisdom of the man upstairs. *Does he really know what he is doing?* they wonder.

The rabbi paused here. We both felt the plane nosing downward. His remaining time was short. But his point was clear. The girl dishonored the name of her father, not with vulgar language, but with insensitive living. Keep this up and the whole building will be second-guessing the CEO.

But my traveling partner wasn't finished. He scratched his bearded chin and lifted both eyebrows as he proposed, "But what if the daughter acted differently?" and then proceeded to recast the story.

Rather than demand a muffin from Bert, she brings a muffin to Bert. "I thought of you this morning," she explains. "You arrive so early. Do you have time to eat?" And she hands him the gift.

En route to the elevator she bumps into a woman with an armful of documents. "My, I'm sorry. Can I help?" the daughter offers. The assistant smiles, and the two carry the stacks down the hallway.

And so the daughter engages the people. She asks about their families, offers to bring them coffee. New workers are welcomed, and hard workers are applauded. She, through kindness and concern, raises the happiness level of the entire company.

She does so not even mentioning her father's name. Never does she declare, "My father says . . . " There is no need to. Is she not his child? Does she not speak on his behalf? Reflect his heart? When she speaks, they assume she speaks for him. And because they think highly of her, they think highly of her father.

They've not seen him.

They've not met him.

But they know his child, so they know his heart.

By now the flight was ending, and so was my Hebrew lesson. Thanks to the rabbi, the third command shouldered new meaning.[1]

MAY WE HAVE NO HIGHER GOAL THAN TO SEE SOMEONE THINK MORE HIGHLY OF OUR FATHER, OUR KING.

Paul, another rabbi, would have appreciated the point. He wrote: "We are ambassadors for Christ, as though God were making an appeal through us" (2 Corinthians 5:20). The ambassador has a singular aim—to represent his king. He promotes the king's agenda, protects the king's reputation, and presents the king's will. The ambassador elevates the name of the king.

May I close this book with a prayer that we do the same? May God rescue us from self-centered thinking. May we have

IT'S NOT ABOUT ME

no higher goal than to see someone think more highly of our Father, our King. After all, it's not about . . . well, you can finish the sentence.

"You know how the story ends?" the rabbi asked as we were taxiing to a stop. Apparently he had a punch line.

"No, I don't. How?"

"The daughter takes the elevator to the top floor to see her father. When she arrives, he is waiting in the doorway. He's aware of her good works and has seen her kind acts. People think more highly of him because of her. And he knows it. As she approaches, he greets her with six words."

The rabbi paused and smiled.

"What are they?" I urged, never expecting to hear an orthodox Jew quote Jesus.

"Well done, good and faithful servant."

May God sustain you until you hear the same.

NOTES

Chapter 3: Divine Self-Promotion

1. Exodus 33:18; 1 Kings 8:10–11; Ezekiel 3:23; Luke 2:9; Hebrews 1:3; John 1:14; Mark 9:1–13; 2 Peter 1:16–18; Matthew 16:27; Revelation 21:23.

Chapter 4: Holy Different

1. Darren Brown, ed., *The Greatest Exploration Stories Ever Told: True Tales of Search and Discovery* (Guilford, Conn.: Lyons Press, 2003), 207–219.
2. Brown, *Greatest Exploration Stories,* 223.
3. Jerry Bridges, *The Pursuit of Holiness* (Colorado Springs, Colo.: NavPress, 1978), 64.
4. Edward W. Goodrick and John R. Kohlenberger, *Zondervan NIV Exhaustive Concordance,* 2d ed., ed. James A. Swanson (Grand Rapids, Mich.: Zondervan Publishing House, 1999), 1487.

Chapter 5: Just a Moment

1. Frederick Buechner, *The Sacred Journey* (San Francisco: Harper and Row, 1982), 9, 37, 76.

Chapter 6: His Unchanging Hand

1. Rick Reilly, "Sportsman of the Year: Lance Armstrong," *Sports Illustrated,* 16 December 2002, 56.

2. Rick Reilly, "The Life of Reilly: Pool Shark," *Sports Illustrated,* 24 March 2003, 126.

3. "Barge Accident Cuts South Padre Island Off from Mainland Texas," http://www.thetimesharebeat.com/archives/2001/ts/ttsept50.htm; "South Padre Island Bridge Collapse," www.bridgepros.com/projects/queenisabellacauseway.

4. J. I. Packer, *Knowing God* (Downers Grove, Ill.: InterVarsity Press, 1973), 71.

Chapter 7: God's Great Love

1. John Bishop, *1041 Sermon Illustrations, Ideas and Expositions,* ed. A. Gordon Nasby (Grand Rapids: Baker Book House, 1952), 213.

2. Rubel Shelly, *The ABCs of the Christian Faith* (Nashville: Wineskins, 1998), 21–22.

Chapter 8: God's Mirrors

1. Dictionary of American Naval Fighting Ships, Office of the Chief of Naval Operations, Naval History

Division, Washington, http://www.ibiblio.org/
hyperwar/USN/ships/dafs/DD/dd400.html.

Chapter 9: My Message Is About Him
   1. Mike Flanagan et al., *The Complete Idiot's Guide to the
       Old West* (New York: Alpha Books, 1999), 171–73.
   2. Rick Atchley, *God's Love Does Not Change,* audio-
       cassette of a sermon, Richland Hills Church of Christ,
       Fort Worth, Texas, 28 July 1996.

Chapter 10: My Salvation Is About Him
   1. Alvin Toffler, *Future Shock* (New York: Bantam Books,
       1970), 222.
   2. James O. Jackson, "The Fatal Dive," *Time,* 28 August
       2000, 30.
   3. J. Alec Motyer et al., *The Message of Philippians*
       (Downers Grove, Ill.: InterVarsity Press, 1984), 166.

Chapter 11: My Body Is About Him
   1. William R. Mattox Jr., "Aha! Call It the Revenge of
       the Church Ladies," *USA Today,* 11 February 1999, 15A.

Chapter 12: My Struggles Are About Him

1. Read a full account of Martin and Gracia's story in Gracia Burnham with Dean Merrill, *In the Presence of My Enemies* (Wheaton, Ill.: Tyndale House, 2003).

Chapter 13: My Success Is About Him

1. Ad Slogans Unlimited, http://www.adslogans.co.uk/hof/hofindx1.html.
2. Anthony de Mello, *Taking Flight: A Book of Story Meditations* (New York: Doubleday, 1988), 99.
3. Tom Knott, "Admiral Deserves a Salute from All," *Washington Times,* 17 June 2003.

Chapter 14: Upward Thinking

1. With appreciation to Rabbi Daniel Thomson for sharing this story.

IT'S NOT ABOUT ME

———

STUDY GUIDE

WRITTEN BY STEVE HALLIDAY

CHAPTER ONE

BUMPING LIFE OFF SELF-CENTER

Beholding

1. What Copernicus did for the earth, God does for our souls. Tapping the collective shoulder of humanity, he points to the Son—his Son—and says, "Behold the center of it all."

   A. Why do you think we naturally look to ourselves as the center of the universe?

   B. How does God reveal his Son as the center of everything?

2. What would happen if we accepted our place as Son reflectors?

   A. What does it mean to be a "Son reflector"?

   B. What do you find most difficult in your role as a "Son reflector"? Why?

3. Life makes sense when we accept our place. The God-centered life works. And it rescues us from a life that doesn't.

   A. How does life make sense when we accept our place? What would you say is your place?

   B. How does a God-centered life rescue us from a life that doesn't work?

Reflecting

1. Read Ephesians 1:18–23.

   A. For what does Paul pray in verse 18? What reason does he give for his prayer in verses 18–19?

B. List the many ways Paul describes Christ in verses 20–23. How does it affect you, personally, that Christ is described in each of these ways?

2. Read 2 Corinthians 3:17–18.

A. How do believers "reflect" the Lord's glory? In what way do they reflect it?

B. What happens as they increasingly reflect God's glory (v. 18)? Who is responsible for this?

CHAPTER TWO
SHOW ME YOUR GLORY

Beholding

1. When our deepest desire is not the things of God, or a favor from God, but God himself, we cross a threshold. Less self-focus, more God-focus. Less about me, more about him.

A. What is your deepest desire? How is this desire reflected in the way you live?

B. Have you crossed the threshold just described? Explain.

2. You and I need what Moses needed—a glimpse of God's glory. Such a sighting can change you forever.

A. Have you ever caught a glimpse of God's glory? If so, describe how and when you made the sighting.

B. Why should a glimpse of God's glory change someone forever?

Reflecting

1. Read Exodus 33:12—34:10.

    A. What instructions does God give Moses in 34:1–4? How do these instructions heighten Moses' anticipation of what is about to happen?

    B. How does God describe himself in 34:5–7? How do the attributes he names contribute to his glory?

    C. How does Moses respond to the revelation of God's glory in 34:8–9? How is this significant for us?

    D. How does God reply to Moses' final request (34:10)? Should this fill us with hope or dread? Why?

2. Read 2 Corinthians 3:7–11.

    A. How does Paul compare and contrast the ministry of Moses with "the ministry of the Spirit"?

    B. In what way was Moses' ministry one "that condemns men" (v. 9 NIV)? If it condemned men, how could it be "glorious"?

    C. Why does the ministry of the Spirit outshine the ministry of Moses (vv. 9–11)?

CHAPTER THREE

DIVINE SELF-PROMOTION

Beholding

1. When you think "God's glory," think "preeminence." And, when you think "preeminence," think "priority." For God's glory is God's priority.

A. How do you display God's preeminence in your own life?

B. Why is God's glory God's priority?

C. Why should God's glory be our priority? When it isn't, why isn't it?

2. God has no ego problem. He does not reveal his glory for his good. We need to witness it for ours.

A. How would you answer someone who complained, "God must be very vain if he's so concerned with everybody seeing his glory"?

B. Why do we need to witness God's glory? How does this help us?

3. Why does the earth spin? For him. Why do you have talents and abilities? For him. Why do you have money or poverty? For him. Strength or struggles? For him. Everything and everyone exists to reveal his glory. Including you.

A. In what ways do you reveal God's glory?

B. In what ways do you think you could better reveal God's glory?

Reflecting

1. Read Exodus 15:11–13.

A. How would you answer the question in verse 11?

B. What does it mean to be "majestic in holiness"?

C. What does it mean to be "awesome in glory" (NIV)?

D. How do God's love and strength comfort and encourage God's people (v. 13)?

2. Read John 12:23–33.

A. How did Jesus expect to be "glorified" (vv. 23–24)?

B. In what way did Jesus expect his followers to mimic his example (vv. 25–26)?

C. Did Jesus look forward with great pleasure to what lay ahead for him (v. 27)? In what did he take ultimate pleasure?

D. How did God put his stamp of approval on Jesus and his mission (v. 29)?

E. How did Jesus picture his mission (vv. 30–33)? In what way was it for the benefit of his followers that he described events like this?

CHAPTER FOUR

HOLY DIFFERENT

Beholding

1. The first and final songs of the Bible magnify the holiness of God.

A. What does "holiness" mean to you? How would you describe it to someone who knew nothing about the Bible?

B. Why do you think the first and final songs of the Bible magnify the holiness of God? What's so important about his holiness?

2. God's holiness silences human boasting.

    A. When are you most tempted to boast?

    B. How does God's holiness silence human boasting?

3. God, who is quick to pardon and full of mercy, purges Isaiah of his sin and redirects his life.

    A. When was the last time you experienced God's quick pardon and fullness of mercy? Describe what happened.

    B. How has God redirected your own life?

Reflecting

1. Read Exodus 15:1–18 and Revelation 15:3–4.

    A. If you were to rewrite the Exodus song to reflect an event in your own life, what would it say?

    B. What is the relationship in the Revelation song between fear and glory and holiness? How does your own life reflect this relationship?

2. Read Isaiah 6:1–8.

    A. How does Isaiah react to this revelation of God's glory (v. 5)? How do you think you would have reacted? Explain.

    B. What resulted from Isaiah's cleansing (v. 8)? How do you think God wants to use Isaiah's experience in your own life?

CHAPTER FIVE

JUST A MOMENT

Beholding

1. God doesn't view history as a progression of centuries but as a single photo. He captures your life, your entire life, in one glance.

   A. How does it make you feel to know that God knows all about you and all about everything that will ever happen to you?

   B. If God really can capture your entire life in a single glance, then what sense does it make to disregard his commands and directions? Why do we often disregard them anyway?

2. Your world extends beyond the barnyard of time. A foreverness woos you.

   A. How does it make you feel to know that you were created as an eternal being?

   B. Describe a time when you felt "foreverness" wooing you.

3. The heavy becomes light when weighed against eternity.

   A. What things feel especially heavy to you right now? How can remembering eternity help to lighten the load?

   B. When you think of eternity, what comes to mind?

Reflecting

1. Read 2 Corinthians 4:13–18.

   A. What hope keeps Paul going (v. 14)?

   B. How does Paul keep from losing heart (v. 16)?

C. What important comparison does Paul make in verse 17?

D. What important life instruction does Paul give in verse 18? How can you follow this instruction in practice?

2. Read Romans 8:18–21.

A. What comparison does Paul make in verse 18? How does this knowledge help him to carry on his work? How can it help you to carry on your work?

B. Who is ultimately behind the story of Planet Earth (v. 20)?

C. To what hope does Paul point us in verse 21?

CHAPTER SIX

His Unchanging Hand

Beholding

1. If you're looking for a place with no change, try a soda machine. With life comes change.

A. How has your life changed in the past year? In the past five years? In the past ten years?

B. How do you expect your life will change in the next year? In the next five years? The next ten years?

C. How do you usually deal with change? Do you generally celebrate it or resist it? Explain.

2. Set your bearings on the one and only North Star in the universe —God. For though life changes, he never does.

A. Are you glad that God doesn't change? Explain.

B. Why is it a good thing that God doesn't change?

3. With change comes the reassuring appreciation of heaven's permanence. God's house will stand forever.

   A. What hope does it give you that God's house will stand forever?

Reflecting

1. Read Malachi 3:6.

   A. What blanket statement does God make in this verse?

   B. What application does God make in light of this truth?

   C. How does God's unchanging nature affect you?

2. Read Hebrews 13:8.

   A. What blanket statement does the writer make in this verse?

   B. How would you describe Jesus as he was "yesterday"?

   C. How is Jesus treating you today as he treated his disciples in the Gospels?

   D. How do you expect Jesus to treat you in the future? Explain.

CHAPTER SEVEN

GOD'S GREAT LOVE

Beholding

1. Does God love you? Behold the cross, and behold your answer.

   A. How does the cross demonstrate God's love for you?

   B. How do difficult times sometimes obscure God's love from our eyes?

2. While you are valuable, you aren't essential. You're important but not indispensable.

    A. Why is it good to know that you're valuable and important? Why is it just as good to know that you're not indispensable?

    B. What would it imply about God if you were both essential and indispensable?

3. To say "It's not about you" is not to say you aren't loved; quite the contrary. It's because God loves you that it's not about you.

    A. How does the fact that "it's not about you" show you God's love?

    B. In what way does the sentiment "It's all about me" demonstrate the essence of sin?

Reflecting

1. Read John 3:13–15.

    A. Why is it important to know where Jesus came from (v. 13)?

    B. What picture does Jesus use to illustrate his own ministry (v. 14; see also Numbers 21:4–9)? What strikes you most about this picture?

    C. How does someone gain eternal life, according to verse 15?

2. Read Ephesians 3:16–19.

    A. What did Paul most want his readers to grasp, according to verse 18?

    B. In what way does God's love surpass knowledge (v. 19)? Have you experienced this to be true? Explain.

C. What was Paul's ultimate prayer for his believing friends (v. 19)? How much of this ultimate desire have you experienced? Explain.

CHAPTER EIGHT

GOD'S MIRRORS

Beholding

1. Reduce the human job description down to one phrase, and this is it: Reflect God's glory.

   A. What does it mean to reflect God's glory?

   B. Describe a time when you knew you provided an excellent reflection of God's glory. What happened?

2. Could it be that the Holy Spirit intentionally selected a verb that would remind us to behold God so intently that we can't help but reflect him?

   A. In what ways do you best behold God?

   B. How does your beholding God enable you to reflect God?

3. He's the source; we are the glass. He's the light; we are the mirrors. He sends the message; we mirror it.

   A. Think of the last time you saw someone forget that God is the source and we are the glass. What happened?

   B. What most stands in the way of you effectively mirroring God's message to others?

Reflecting

1. Read Romans 2:17–24.

   A. What advantages does Paul list for his fellow Jews in verses 17–20? Do you recognize any of these advantages in your own life? Explain.

   B. What challenge does Paul give in verses 21–23? Why does he give this challenge?

   C. What warning does Paul issue in verse 24? How is this warning relevant to us today? What does it have to do with reflecting God?

2. Read 1 Corinthians 10:31.

   A. How does someone drink to the glory of God?

   B. How does someone eat to the glory of God?

   C. How can doing everything to the glory of God change not only what you do, but how you do it?

CHAPTER NINE

MY MESSAGE IS ABOUT HIM

Beholding

1. Paul existed to deliver the message. How people remembered him was secondary. (Else why would he introduce himself as a slave?)

   A. Why do you think Paul so often introduced himself as a slave? Whose slave was he?

   B. Would you describe yourself as a slave? Explain.

2. I believe Satan trains battalions of demons to whisper one question in our ears: "What are people thinking of you?"

   A. Why do we care so much what people might be thinking of us?

   B. How can we train ourselves not to listen to Satan's battalions of demons?

3. God doesn't need you and me to do his work. We are expedient messengers, ambassadors by his kindness, not by our cleverness.

   A. What does it mean to be an ambassador by his kindness?

   B. What kind of an ambassador for God are you? Do most people know who you represent? And if so, what do they generally think of him?

Reflecting

1. Read Matthew 6:1–4.

   A. What temptation do we often face when we do a kind thing for someone else, according to verse 1? What instruction does Jesus give us? What warning?

   B. How do we sometimes announce our charitable acts with "trumpets" (vv. 2–4)? How does Jesus instruct us to proceed instead? What promise does he give for those who heed his words?

   C. What do all of these verses have to do with God's glory and God's message?

2. Read 1 Corinthians 1:18–31.

  A. What groups does Paul contrast throughout this passage? Why does he build such a contrast?

  B. Why do any of us receive God's mercy and grace, according to verse 30?

  C. Who alone is fit to boast, according to verse 31? About what should these individuals boast? Why?

CHAPTER TEN

My Salvation Is About Him

Beholding

1. The work of Christ is the bungee cord for the soul. Trust it and take the plunge.

  A. In what way is the work of Christ the bungee cord for the soul?

  B. How do you trust the work of Christ and take the plunge?

2. Legalism discounts God and in the process makes a mess out of us.

  A. How does legalism discount God?

  B. How does legalism make a mess out of us?

3. Your salvation showcases God's mercy. It makes nothing of your effort but everything of his.

  A. How does your salvation make "nothing" of your effort? How does it make "everything" of God's effort?

  B. How do some of us try to add other things to the work of Christ?

Reflecting

1. Read Isaiah 48:10–11.

   A. How does God describe his care of his people in verse 10? Can you identify with this? Explain.

   B. What reason does God give in verse 11 for his actions? Why does he go to such great lengths to purify a people for his own?

2. Read Philippians 3:7–11.

   A. How much did Paul lose because of his connection to Christ (v. 8)? How did he feel about this loss?

   B. How does Paul describe his righteousness in verse 9? Where does this new standing come from?

   C. How does Paul describe his greatest hope in verses 10–11? Does this describe your own greatest hope? Explain.

CHAPTER ELEVEN

MY BODY IS ABOUT HIM

Beholding

1. The me-centered phrase "as long as no one gets hurt" sounds noble, but the truth is, we don't know who gets hurt.

   A. Why is the phrase "as long as no one gets hurt" described as "me-centered"?

   B. Why don't we know who gets hurt?

2. Casual sex is a diet of chocolate—it tastes good for a while, but

the imbalance can ruin you. Sex apart from God's plan wounds the soul.

    A. How can casual sex ruin a person? What "imbalance" is meant here?

    B. Why does sex apart from God's plan wound the soul?

3. Manage God's house in such a way that passersby stop and notice. "Who lives in that house?" they will ask. And when they hear the answer, God will be honored.

    A. When was the last time anyone asked you the equivalent of "Who lives in your house"? Explain.

    B. How is God honored when we are asked such a question?

Reflecting

1. Read 1 Corinthians 6:12–13.

    A. What guideline does Paul use to manage his freedom in Christ (v. 12)?

    B. How does verse 13 point to a future event that ought to shape how we live today?

    C. For what is the body meant, according to verse 13? What does this mean?

    D. How can you honor God with your own body?

2. Read Romans 6:12–14.

    A. How can you refuse to "let" sin reign in your body?

    B. How do we sometimes offer the parts of our body to sin?

C. In what way can sin become our master? How can we depend on God's grace to make sure this doesn't happen?

CHAPTER TWELVE

MY STRUGGLES ARE ABOUT HIM

Beholding

1. Can't the Maker of heaven and earth handle bad traffic and prevent bad marriages? Of course he can. Then why doesn't he?

   A. Describe the last time you wondered why God didn't intervene to stop some sad event. What answer did you come up with?

   B. How would you answer someone who asked the question above?

2. Don't blame suffering in the world on the anger of God. He's not mad; he didn't mess up. Follow our troubles to their headwaters, and you won't find an angry or befuddled God. But you will find a sovereign God.

   A. What does it mean to you that God is sovereign?

   B. If God is sovereign, then why shouldn't we blame him for the suffering in the world?

3. Rather than begrudge your problem, explore it. Ponder it. And most of all, use it. Use it to the glory of God.

   A. What does it mean to explore your problem rather than begrudge it?

B. What problem do you have right now that you could use to the glory of God? How could it be so used?

Reflecting

1. Read John 9:1–38.

    A. How is the question asked in verse 2 very much like some questions still asked today?

    B. How does Jesus answer the question? In what way must his answer have greatly surprised the crowd?

    C. How does the man respond to Jesus (v. 38)? In what way did this glorify God?

2. Read John 11:1–45.

    A. How does Jesus respond to the message about Lazarus (vv. 4–6)? Why does he respond like this?

    B. Did Mary and Martha understand Jesus' words in verse 23? How about in verses 38–40?

    C. In what way is the crowd's question in verse 37 still being asked today about all kinds of tragedies?

    D. How did Jesus' disciples, friends, and others see God's glory, as Jesus promised in verses 4 and 40?

    E. What was the result of seeing God's glory (v. 45)?

CHAPTER THIRTEEN

MY SUCCESS IS ABOUT HIM

Beholding

1. When foreigners saw the fruitful farms of the Promised Land, God did not want them to think about the farmer but the farmer's Maker. Their success advertised God.

    A. Does your own success advertise God? Explain.

    B. Who in your acquaintance best advertises God? How does he or she do this?

2. They failed at success. They forgot both the source and purpose of their success.

    A. How is it possible to fail at success? Have you ever done so? Explain.

    B. How do you remind yourself of the source and purpose of your success?

3. Why are you good at what you do? For God's sake. Your success is not about what you do. It's all about him—his present and future glory.

    A. What are you good at? How do you use what you're good at for God's sake?

    B. How does what you do advertise God's glory? How can it advertise God's future glory?

Reflecting

1. Read Deuteronomy 8:6–18.

   A. How did God instruct his people to respond to their good fortune (v. 10)? Is this still a good idea? Why?

   B. What warning did God give his people (vv. 11–14)? Does it still apply today? Why or why not?

   C. What forecast does God give in verse 17? Why does he give it?

2. Read Psalm 44:1–3.

   A. What does the psalmist remember in the first two verses? Why is it important to remember such things?

   B. What lesson does the psalmist teach in verse 3? Why is this lesson always important to keep in mind?

   C. Why did God give his people victory, according to verse 3? Can this same truth give us victory today? Explain.

CHAPTER FOURTEEN

UPWARD THINKING

Beholding

1. The girl dishonored the name of her father, not with vulgar language, but with insensitive living. Keep this up and the whole building will be second-guessing the CEO.

   A. How does insensitive living on the part of God's children cause people to second-guess God?

B. What issues of insensitive living do you struggle with the most? How can you best deal with these issues?

2. May God rescue us from self-centered thinking. May we have no higher goal than to see someone think more highly of our Father, our King.

  A. In what areas of life is it easiest for you to slip into self-centered thinking?

  B. What practical steps can you take today to help others think more highly of your God than they do of you?

Reflecting

1. Read Exodus 20:7.

  A. How have you normally interpreted this commandment?

  B. Why is God so concerned with the use of his name?

2. Read Matthew 25:14–23.

  A. Why is it important to know that the master was gone "a long time" (v. 19)?

  B. How does the master respond to the first two servants (vv. 20–23)?

  C. How can you be like either of the first two servants? Do you expect one day to hear words similar to those they heard? Explain.

OUTLIVE YOUR LIFE

MAX LUCADO

CHAPTER ONE

OUR ONCE-IN-HISTORY OPPORTUNITY

By the time you knew what to call it, you were neck deep in it. You'd toddler walked and talked, smelled crayons and swung bats, gurgled and giggled your way out of diapers and into childhood.

You'd noticed how guys aren't gals and dogs aren't cats and pizza sure beats spinach. And then, somewhere in the midst of it all, it hit you. At your grandpa's funeral perhaps. Maybe when you waved good-bye as your big brother left for the marines. You realized that these days are more than ice cream trips, homework, and pimples. This is called life. And this one is yours.

Complete with summers and songs and gray skies and tears, you have a life. Didn't request one, but you have one. A first day. A final day. And a few thousand in between. You've been given an honest-to-goodness human life.

You've been given your life. No one else has your version. You'll never bump into yourself on the sidewalk. You'll never meet anyone who has your exact blend of lineage, loves, and longings. Your life will never be lived by anyone else. You're not a jacket in an attic that can be recycled after you are gone.

And who pressed the accelerator? As soon as one day is lived, voilà, here comes another. The past has passed, and the good old days are exactly that: old days, the stuff of rearview mirrors and scrapbooks. Life is racing past, and if we aren't careful, you and I will look up, and our shot at it will have passed us by.

Some people don't bother with such thoughts. They grind through their days without lifting their eyes to look. They live and die and never ask why.

But you aren't numbered among them, or you wouldn't be holding a book entitled *Outlive Your Life*. It's not enough for you to do well. You want to do good. You want your life to matter. You want to live in such a way that the world will be glad you did.

But how can you? How can I? Can God use us?

I have one hundred and twenty answers to that question. One hundred and twenty residents of ancient Israel. They were the charter members of the Jerusalem church (Acts 1:15). Fishermen, some. Revenue reps, others. A former streetwalker and a converted revolutionary or two. They had no clout with Caesar, no friends at the temple headquarters. Truth be told, they had nothing more than this: a fire in the belly to change the world.

Thanks to Luke, we know how they fared. He recorded their stories in the book of Acts. Let's listen to it. That's right—*listen* to the book of Acts. It cracks with the sounds of God's ever-expanding work. Press your ear against the pages, and hear God press into the corners and crevices of the world.

Hear sermons echo off the temple walls. Baptismal waters splashing, just-saved souls laughing. Hear the spoon scrape the bowl as yet another hungry mouth is fed.

Listen to the doors opening and walls collapsing. Doors to Antioch, Ethiopia, Corinth, and Rome. Doors into palaces, prisons, and Roman courts.

And walls. The ancient prejudice between Jew and Samaritan—down! The thick and spiked division between Jew and Gentile—crash! The partitions that quarantined male from female, landowner from pauper, master from slave, black African from Mediterranean Jew—God demolishes them all.

Acts announces, "God is afoot!"

Is he still? we wonder. *Would God do with us what he did with his first followers?*

Heaven knows we hope so. These are devastating times: 3 billion people are desperately poor, 1 billion are hungry, millions are trafficked in slavery, and pandemic diseases are gouging entire nations. Each year more than 2 million children are exploited in the global commercial sex trade.[1] And in the five minutes it took you to read these pages, almost 90 children died of preventable diseases.[2] More than half of all Africans do not have access to modern health facilities. As a result, 10 million of them die each year from diarrhea, acute respiratory

---

1. "Sex Trafficking and Commercial Sexual Exploitation," International Justice Mission, http://www.ijm.org.
2. That equals approximately 25,000 per day. "Today, over 25,000 Children Died around the World," Global Issues, http://www.globalissues.org/article/715/today-over-25000-children-died-around-the-world.

illness, malaria, and measles. Many of those deaths could be prevented by one shot.[3]

Yet in the midst of the wreckage, here we stand, the modern-day version of the Jerusalem church. You, me, and our one-of-a-kind lifetimes and once-in-history opportunity.

Ours is the wealthiest generation of Christians ever. We are bright, educated, and experienced. We can travel around the world in twenty-four hours or send a message in a millisecond. We have the most sophisticated research and medicines at the tips of our fingers. We have ample resources. A mere 2 percent of the world's grain harvest would be enough, if shared, to erase the problems of hunger and malnutrition around the world.[4] There is enough food on the planet to offer every person twenty-five hundred calories of sustenance a day.[5] We have enough food to feed the hungry.

And we have enough bedrooms to house the orphans. Here's the math. Projections indicated that by 2010 there would be 106 million orphans worldwide.[6] More than 159 million people in the United States call themselves Christians.[7] From a purely statistical standpoint, American Christians by

3. Peter Greer and Phil Smith, *The Poor Will Be Glad: Joining the Revolution to Lift the World Out of Poverty* (Grand Rapids: Zondervan, 2009), 26.
4. Ronald J. Sider, *Rich Christians in an Age of Hunger: Moving from Affluence to Generosity* (Nashville: Thomas Nelson, 2005), 10.
5. Sider, *Rich Christians*, 35.
6. U.S. Agency for International Development, *Children on the Brink 2002: A Joint Report on Orphan Estimates and Program Strategies*, http://www.usaid.gov/our_work/global_health/aids/Publications/docs/childrenbrink.pdf.
7. "Largest Religious Groups in the United States of America," Adherents.com, www.adherents.com/rel_USA.html.

themselves have the wherewithal to house every orphan in the world.

Of course, many people are not in a position to do so. They are elderly, infirm, unemployed, or simply feel no call to adopt. Yet what if a small percentage of them did? A percentage of, hmmm, let's say 7.5. If so, we could provide loving homes for the more than 11 million children in sub-Saharan Africa who have been orphaned by the AIDS epidemic.[8] Among the noble causes of the church, how does that one sound? "American Christians Stand Up for AIDS Orphans." Wouldn't that headline be a welcome one?

I don't mean to oversimplify these terribly complicated questions. We can't just snap our fingers and expect the grain to flow across borders or governments to permit foreign adoptions. Policies stalemate the best of efforts. International relations are strained. Corrupt officials snag the systems. I get that.

But this much is clear: the storehouse is stocked. The problem is not in the supply; the problem is in the distribution. God has given this generation, *our generation*, everything we need to alter the course of human suffering.

A few years back, three questions rocked my world. They came from different people in the span of a month. Question 1: Had you been a German Christian during World War II, would you have taken a stand against Hitler? Question 2: Had you lived in the South during the civil rights conflict, would

---

8. "Fact Sheet: The Global AIDS Crisis," World Vision, http://www.worldvision.org/content.nsf/about/press-development-aids-factsheet?Open&lpos=lft_txt_Global-AIDS-Factsheet.

you have taken a stand against racism? Question 3: When your grandchildren discover you lived during a day in which 3 billion people were poor and 1 billion were hungry, how will they judge your response?

I didn't mind the first two questions. They were hypothetical. I'd like to think I would have taken a stand against Hitler and fought against racism. But those days are gone, and those choices were not mine. But the third question has kept me awake at night. I do live today; so do you. We are given a choice . . . an opportunity to make a big difference during a difficult time. What if we did? What if we rocked the world with hope? Infiltrated all corners with God's love and life? What if we followed the example of the Jerusalem church? This tiny sect expanded into a world-changing force. We still drink from their wells and eat from their trees of faith. How did they do it? What can we learn from their priorities and passion?

Let's ponder their stories, found in the first twelve chapters of Acts. Let's examine each event through the lens of this prayer: *Do it again, Jesus. Do it again.* After all, "We are God's masterpiece. He has created us anew in Christ Jesus, so we can do the good things he planned for us long ago" (Ephesians 2:10 NLT). We are created by a great God to do great works. He invites us to outlive our lives, not just in heaven but here on earth.

Here's a salute to a long life: goodness that outlives the grave, love that outlasts the final breath. May you live in such a way that your death is just the beginning of your life.